Learning Xamarin Studio

Learn how to build high-performance native applications using the power of Xamarin Studio

William Smith

BIRMINGHAM - MUMBAI

Learning Xamarin Studio

Copyright © 2014 Packt Publishing

All rights reserved. No part of this book may be reproduced, stored in a retrieval system, or transmitted in any form or by any means, without the prior written permission of the publisher, except in the case of brief quotations embedded in critical articles or reviews.

Every effort has been made in the preparation of this book to ensure the accuracy of the information presented. However, the information contained in this book is sold without warranty, either express or implied. Neither the author, nor Packt Publishing, and its dealers and distributors will be held liable for any damages caused or alleged to be caused directly or indirectly by this book.

Packt Publishing has endeavored to provide trademark information about all of the companies and products mentioned in this book by the appropriate use of capitals. However, Packt Publishing cannot guarantee the accuracy of this information.

First published: August 2014

Production reference: 1120814

Published by Packt Publishing Ltd.
Livery Place
35 Livery Street
Birmingham B3 2PB, UK.

ISBN 978-1-78355-081-4

www.packtpub.com

Cover image by Gerard Eykhoff (gerard@eykhoff.nl)

Credits

Author
William Smith

Reviewers
Ryan Alford
John Goodwin
Matt Kennedy
Sergio Martínez-Losa del Rincón
Carlo Wahlstedt

Commissioning Editor
Amarabha Banerjee

Acquisition Editor
Sam Wood

Content Development Editor
Mohammed Fahad

Technical Editor
Pratik More

Copy Editors
Roshni Banerjee
Adithi Shetty

Project Coordinator
Danuta Jones

Proofreader
Simran Bhogal

Indexers
Hemangini Bari
Mariammal Chettiyar

Production Coordinator
Arvindkumar Gupta

Cover Work
Arvindkumar Gupta

About the Author

William Smith has been writing on software since 1988, when his parents asked him to make a choice between a school-sponsored trip to Europe (which his elder sister was enjoying at the time), or a computer. Although accused of being short-sighted, William chose the computer and he firmly believes he got the better deal. He began writing about software on the Tandy 1000 SL/2 using Turbo C++ and has been hooked on the technology ever since.

He began his professional career in the environmental field eight years later with degrees in Environmental Science and Business Administration. While working in this field full-time, he started his first business focused on installing and managing small commercial networks and websites. In this role, he saw a need for specialized network analysis tools, so he learned VB.NET and wrote simple console applications for his own use. From there, he continued writing applications as a hobbyist before returning to the University of Maryland for a second Bachelor's degree in Computer Science. While still completing the Computer Science program, he was offered a position with a software development firm based in Pittsburgh, PA, where he spent the next few years working with .NET and Xamarin developing iOS applications. As a result of this experience, he was asked to be a technical reviewer for *iOS Development with Xamarin Cookbook, Dimitris Tavlikos, Packt Publishing*.

William currently works for GIS Inc. in Birmingham, AL, as a Geospatial Developer specializing in native mobile application development. He also owns Websmiths, LLC (www.websmithsllc.com), a consulting firm concentrating on cross-platform mobile application development using Xamarin Studio.

He lives in wild and wonderful West Virginia with his beautiful wife and four sons. He enjoys hunting and fishing with his family, and he still hasn't been to Europe.

> I want to thank the Lord Jesus Christ for giving me the opportunity to write this book. I would also like to thank my wife Dorothy for her support and my family for their patience with me as I completed this work.

About the Reviewers

Ryan Alford is a .NET software engineer who works from home. He has been a .NET developer for over 7 years, with majority of his focus being on C#. In his early years, he worked almost exclusively on WinForms and Windows Mobile. He then started working with ASP.NET, AJAX, and Silverlight. In the past few years, as mobile development really started to take off, he took an interest in Xamarin and MonoTouch.

He was able to help convince management at his workplace to use Xamarin for their upcoming enterprise application on iOS, since the company was using .NET and C# in other projects. It was at this point that he was added to the three-person development team to write the new iOS enterprise application.

He has written and released two Android applications: MotoTorch LED and Phase 10 Score Center. MotoTorch LED has more than 500,000 downloads, and was one of the first applications on Android that used the camera LEDs as a flashlight.

Today, Ryan is rewriting Phase 10 Score Center in Xamarin.Android to ease the development of new features. He is still on his iOS team and continues to add new features to his company's enterprise application.

John Goodwin was born in 1979 on South Korean soil as an American citizen to US Army parents. He moved a lot with his family, eventually spending much of his youth in Washington State.

After meeting his wife Jane, he moved to California, where he soon became employed as a professional software developer for a company in Canoga Park, CA, known as Cyberspace Headquarters, LLC. Working there for several years, he progressed from the lowly new guy to Lead Software Developer, in charge of two, or sometimes three other software developers as well as offshore development projects. The economic downturn for IT companies post 9/11 eventually took its toll, and John looked elsewhere for employment, and also moved with his wife further out of the city.

Next in rural Northern Los Angeles County, he took some teaching opportunities. Then he worked short-term for a Simi Valley factory looking to improve worker efficiencies. Soon, an opening in the City of Los Angeles for a contract software developer made its way to his ears; he interviewed, and started work.

In the housing boom from 2002-2006, it had already been very clear that Southern California's bubble was about to burst. John and Jane sold their home in favor of moving to Lake Royale, where he continued to work for the City of Los Angeles telecommute. After working 7 years for the City of Los Angeles, he started working at CareAnyware doing healthcare-related software for home health and hospice. CareAnyware was soon purchased by Brightree, where he continues to work writing post-acute healthcare software with great immediate teammates and remote teams.

His passion for using technology to create value in the lives of others is mysteriously tolerated by his loving wife. Unable to find a normal way to work out and keep fit, he uses local sprint triathlons (and maybe a half in October 2014) to motivate his workout schedule. You can visit his website: `http://johngoodwin.com/`

I want to thank my brother and family, mother, and stepfather for their contribution to the family support structure.

Sergio Martínez-Losa del Rincón is a computer engineer who loves programming languages. Since high school, he has been learning about programming and computer interaction. He is always learning and discovers something new every day.

He likes all kinds of programming languages, but focuses his efforts into mobile development with native languages such as Objective-C (iPhone), Java (Android), and Xamarin (C#). He also builds Google Glass applications at his job as well as mobile applications for iPhone and Android devices. He also develops games for mobile devices with Cocos2d-x and cocos2d. He has reviewed *Learning Cocos2d-x Game Development, Siddarth Shekar, Packt Publishing*.

He loves challenging problems and is always keen to work with new technologies. More information about his experience and details can be found at `www.linkedin.com/in/sergiomtzlosa`.

Carlo Wahlstedt is a graduate from Berea College. He has been a professional software engineer since 2007, with a focus on the .NET Framework. He has held jobs in the utility and financial industries. He has earned a Microsoft Certified Solutions Developer: Web Applications certification and has been very actively working with Xamarin Studio for over a year. He is most interested in software for the Web and mobile devices, as well as software development processes and wearable technology.

www.PacktPub.com

Support files, eBooks, discount offers, and more

You might want to visit www.PacktPub.com for support files and downloads related to your book.

Did you know that Packt offers eBook versions of every book published, with PDF and ePub files available? You can upgrade to the eBook version at www.PacktPub.com and as a print book customer, you are entitled to a discount on the eBook copy. Get in touch with us at service@packtpub.com for more details.

At www.PacktPub.com, you can also read a collection of free technical articles, sign up for a range of free newsletters and receive exclusive discounts and offers on Packt books and eBooks.

http://PacktLib.PacktPub.com

Do you need instant solutions to your IT questions? PacktLib is Packt's online digital book library. Here, you can access, read and search across Packt's entire library of books.

Why subscribe?

- Fully searchable across every book published by Packt
- Copy and paste, print and bookmark content
- On demand and accessible via web browser

Free access for Packt account holders

If you have an account with Packt at www.PacktPub.com, you can use this to access PacktLib today and view nine entirely free books. Simply use your login credentials for immediate access.

Table of Contents

Preface	**1**
Chapter 1: Installing and Setting Up Xamarin Studio	**7**
Xamarin Studio pricing plans	**8**
Starter	8
Indie	8
Business	9
Enterprise	9
Understanding the pricing structure	9
An example company	10
Xamarin Studio platform options	**10**
Xamarin.Android	11
Xamarin.iOS	11
Xamarin.Mac	11
Installing development components	**11**
Installing Xcode and the iOS SDK	**12**
Installing Xcode from the App Store	12
Installing Xcode manually	13
Finishing the Xcode installation	14
Installing Xamarin Studio	**14**
Apple Developer Program	**17**
Google Play Developer Program	**19**
Setting up simulators and emulators	**20**
iOS simulators	21
Android emulators	22
Creating a Nexus 7 AVD using the AVD Manager	22
Creating a Samsung Galaxy S4 AVD using the SDK and AVD Manager	23
Improving AVD performance	**26**
Intel x86 Atom System Image	26
Hardware Acceleration Execution Manager	27

Run from Snapshot	29
Third-party AVD options	30
Setting up test devices	**30**
Setting up iOS devices	31
Obtaining a development certificate	31
Provisioning your devices	32
Setting up Android devices	33
Enabling debugging on your device	33
Installing USB drivers and connecting your device	34
Setting up source control	**35**
Additional resources for cross-platform developers	**37**
Xamarin resources	37
Third-party resources	37
Summary	**38**
Chapter 2: Learning and Customizing the XS Environment	**39**
The Xamarin Studio IDE	**40**
Creating your first iOS application	**41**
Creating your first Android application	**42**
The Solution pad	**42**
Design pads	**43**
Information pads	**44**
Application, File, and Edit menus	**46**
View and Search menus	**48**
The Project menu	**50**
Build and Run menus	**51**
The Version Control menu	**54**
Tools, Window, and Help menus	**56**
Solution Options	**57**
The General group	58
The Build and Run groups	58
The Source Code group	58
The Version Control group	58
Project Options	**59**
The General group	59
The Build group	60
iOS-specific panes	61
Android-specific panes	64
The Run group	67
Source Code and Version Control groups	68
Environment preferences	**68**
Environment	69
Projects	69

Text Editor	69
Source Code, Version Control, Other, and Packages groups	70
Summary	**71**
Chapter 3: Working with Xcode and the Android SDK	**73**
Introduction to Xcode	**74**
Toolbar	75
The navigator area	75
The utility area	77
The debug area	79
The editor area	79
Outlets and Actions	**80**
Outlets	81
Actions	81
Adding Outlets and Actions	82
Adding a ViewController to our project	**83**
How it works	84
XIB, NIB, DESIGNER, and STORYBOARD files	**85**
Xamarin Studio Designer for iOS	**87**
Creating a storyboard in Xamarin Studio	**88**
How it works	91
Android SDK Manager	**92**
Android Layouts	94
Xamarin Studio Designer for Android	**95**
Creating a Layout in Xamarin Studio	**96**
How it works	97
Summary	**99**
Chapter 4: Plugins, Templates, Libraries, and Files	**101**
Installing the Visual Studio plugin	**102**
Configuring your Mac	103
Configuring your Windows machine	103
Configuring a Windows VM within Mac	104
Final installation steps	105
Configuring the Visual Studio toolbar	105
Creating an iPhone application in Visual Studio	**106**
How it works	109
Project templates	**110**
iOS project templates	110
Android project templates	113
Mac and Mac (open source) project templates	114

Libraries	**115**
Portable Class Library	115
Binding Project	116
iOS Binding Project	116
Java Bindings Library	117
Files	**117**
Summary	**121**
Chapter 5: Working with Xamarin.Forms	**123**
Requirements for using Xamarin.Forms	124
The Xamarin.Forms project templates	124
The components of Xamarin.Forms	125
Data binding	125
Components	125
Navigation	126
The API design	126
How it works	133
The XAML design	135
How it works	141
Summary	**142**
Chapter 6: Application Lifecycle	**143**
The iOS application lifecycle	144
The AppDelegate class	145
UIViewController lifecycle methods	147
Examining iOS lifecycles	148
Examining the application lifecycle	149
The Android application lifecycle	150
Understanding application lifecycle	150
Activity lifecycle methods	152
Configuration changes	155
Examining application states	155
Examining the Activity lifecycle	156
The background state	157
Summary	**159**
Chapter 7: Testing and Debugging	**161**
The Xamarin debugger	162
Unit tests	163
Touch.Unit and Andr.Unit	164
Creating a unit test project	164
Running the tests	166
How it works	168

Simulators	**169**
Testing in an iOS simulator	**170**
Running the tests	172
How it works	173
Testing in an Android emulator	**174**
Running the tests	175
How it works	176
Device testing	**176**
Testing on an iOS device	177
Testing on an Android device	177
TestFlight	**178**
Setting up a TestFlight account	178
Instruments	**179**
Device Monitor	**180**
Logs	**180**
Other testing considerations	**181**
Summary	**182**
Chapter 8: Deployment	**183**
Deploying iOS applications	**184**
Distribution provisioning profile	185
Generating a production certificate signing request	185
Submitting a production certificate signing request	187
Creating the App ID	188
Creating and installing the distribution profile	188
Build configuration	189
Bundle signing	190
Publishing your application	190
Setting up an iTunes Connect account	191
Creating the application page	191
Uploading the binary	194
Deploying Mac applications	**195**
Installing Developer Certificates	196
Registering a Mac App ID	196
Creating a Mac App Development certificate	197
Creating Mac App Store Certificates	198
Creating a Developer ID Certificate	199
Registering the Mac OS X development machine	199
Creating the development provisioning profiles	200
Creating the production provisioning profiles	201
Setting the app configuration	201
Signing your application for direct deployment	202
Build for direct deployment	203

Signing your application for deployment to the Mac App Store	203
Build for Mac App Store deployment	204
Deploying to the Mac App Store	205
Deploying Android applications	**208**
Preparing your application for release compile	208
Creating a private keystore	210
Signing the APK	211
Publishing to the Google Play Store	212
Summary	**215**
Appendix: Images and Graphics Tables	**217**
iOS application icons	**217**
iOS 3.5-inch Retina display screenshots	**218**
iOS 4-inch Retina display screenshots	**218**
iOS iPad screenshots	**219**
Mac OS X app screenshots	**219**
Android application icons	**220**
Android screenshots	**220**
Index	**221**

Preface

There are a number of options available for the developer who wants to create cross-platform mobile applications. The most obvious solution is to go native and develop on the platform directly, and this approach has some very significant advantages. For one, nothing is going to run as fast and efficiently as a native app. Also, your applications will have full access to everything the OS and hardware have to offer. However, cross-platform native development presents a serious complication—multiple platforms mean multiple applications written in multiple languages, possibly even by multiple development teams.

This was painfully true a few years ago, but not any longer. Now we have Xamarin Studio that allows us to use one technology to create native applications for multiple platforms. All of our work can be built using .NET, so there's no need to learn Objective-C or Java, or have multiple applications and development teams.

As is the case with any new tool or technology, installing and integrating Xamarin Studio into your workflow takes time. The purpose of this book is to remove the guesswork from that process by walking through the most complex and confusing portions. We'll begin with a detailed walkthrough of installing and configuring Xamarin Studio. This walkthrough will include integrating third-party software and tools, setting up your developer accounts, setting up simulators and emulators, and preparing your physical devices for testing. Next, we'll take a detailed look at the IDE itself including basic functionality, environment variables, and user preferences. Finally, we'll look at how to use Xamarin Studio to deploy your applications. This will include a review of the various testing tools available in Xamarin Studio, and a walkthrough of the actual deployment process to several application marketplaces.

So, for the moment, please ignore the fanatics who insist that C, memory pointers, and manual memory management are the tools that define a "real" programmer. Your average users (paying customers) don't care what language or technology you built the app on; they care about more practical things. Does the app have a clean UI with a user friendly workflow? Is the app consistent and reliable? Is the app fast? Does the app meet my needs at a fair price? Apps built with Xamarin Studio can answer yes to all of these questions just as readily as an app built using a native language.

What this book covers

Chapter 1, *Installing and Setting Up Xamarin Studio*, begins by introducing the Xamarin licensing options available for purchase. Next, it will help you get started by walking you through the process of installing the Xamarin Studio and Xcode IDEs, setting up Apple and Google developer accounts, and installing the Android SDK Manager. Using these tools, you will walk through the process of setting up simulators, emulators, and devices for testing. Finally, this chapter will demonstrate setting up source control through Xamarin Studio.

Chapter 2, *Learning and Customizing the XS Environment*, will walk you through creating your first iOS and Android application using Xamarin Studio. Using the development of these applications as a context, you will learn about the various menus and features of the Xamarin Studio IDE. You will also learn about solution and project-level properties, as well as the environmental preferences you can use to customize your personal development workflow.

Chapter 3, *Working with Xcode and the Android SDK*, explains the key features and functions of Xcode and the Android SDK. A discussion on every aspect of these tools is beyond the scope of this book, unfortunately. Instead, this chapter will focus only on the critical functions necessary for Xamarin developers to successfully accomplish their cross-platform development goals.

Chapter 4, *Plugins, Templates, Libraries, and Files*, begins by introducing the Visual Studio plugin, and then explains how to connect to a networked Mac build machine. Following this, the various projects, libraries, and file types available for your applications are explained in detail. With a basic understanding of these components well in hand, you will be ready to explore how these components can be applied in your applications.

Chapter 5, *Working with Xamarin.Forms*, will introduce you to the Xamarin.Forms framework provided in Xamarin 3. By following the walkthroughs provided, you will build a fully functional cross-platform application in just a few minutes using XAML and the UI design API included with the framework.

Chapter 6, *Application Lifecycle*, details application states and application lifecycles for iOS and Android applications. This discussion might seem out of place in a book intended to introduce a development tool, but an understanding of this material is absolutely critical to successfully use Xamarin Studio to develop cross-platform mobile applications.

Chapter 7, *Testing and Debugging*, discusses the tools available in Xamarin Studio for testing including unit test projects, debugging tools, simulators and emulators, crash logs, TestFlight, and testing on physical devices. Additionally, two platform-specific suites of powerful testing tools are also discussed.

Chapter 8, *Deployment*, brings it all together by walking through the process of releasing your apps to the Apple and Google App Stores. In this chapter, you will learn how to use Xamarin Studio and other tools and utilities to create provisioning profiles and build configurations, bundle signing, and building for deployment. You will also learn about platform-specific tasks such as how to use iTunes Connect to release your application directly to the iStore.

Appendix, *Images and Graphics Tables*, details the specifications for images and graphics required to upload your finished applications to select marketplaces.

What you need for this book

To get the most from this book, you will need an active Internet connection to download the various components required to set up the development environment. Also, several of the examples will require an active Apple or Google Developer account.

In order to run the example code in this book, you will need, at a minimum, a PC running Windows 7 or higher and any non-Express version of Visual Studio 2010, 2012, or 2013. Additionally, if you intend to perform iOS or Mac development work, you will need a Mac running OS X Lion or higher. This Mac can be used as either a primary development environment, or can be paired with a PC to act as a networked build machine.

Who this book is for

If you are a developer who wants to get started using Xamarin Studio for cross-platform development with .NET, this is the book for you. Developers of any skill level or background will find this book useful to set up their development environment and learn to navigate the IDE. Some degree of programming knowledge, ideally in .NET languages, is assumed but not required.

Conventions

In this book, you will find a number of styles of text that distinguish between different kinds of information. Here are some examples of these styles, and an explanation of their meaning.

Code words in text, database table names, folder names, filenames, file extensions, pathnames, dummy URLs, user input, and Twitter handles are shown as follows: "Open the `HelloiPhoneViewController.cs` file."

A block of code is set as follows:

```
#if DEBUG
[assembly: Application(Debuggable=true)]
#else
[assembly: Application(Debuggable=false)]
#endif
```

New terms and **important words** are shown in bold. Words that you see on the screen, in menus or dialog boxes for example, appear in the text like this: "The **General** pane allows you to define parameters, decide whether or not your app should run on an external console."

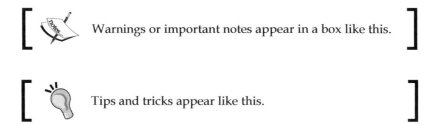

> Warnings or important notes appear in a box like this.

> Tips and tricks appear like this.

Reader feedback

Feedback from our readers is always welcome. Let us know what you think about this book—what you liked or may have disliked. Reader feedback is important for us to develop titles that you really get the most out of.

To send us general feedback, simply send an e-mail to `feedback@packtpub.com`, and mention the book title via the subject of your message.

If there is a topic that you have expertise in and you are interested in either writing or contributing to a book, see our author guide on `www.packtpub.com/authors`.

Customer support

Now that you are the proud owner of a Packt book, we have a number of things to help you to get the most from your purchase.

Downloading the example code

You can download the example code files for all Packt books you have purchased from your account at http://www.packtpub.com. If you purchased this book elsewhere, you can visit http://www.packtpub.com/support and register to have the files e-mailed directly to you.

Errata

Although we have taken every care to ensure the accuracy of our content, mistakes do happen. If you find a mistake in one of our books—maybe a mistake in the text or the code—we would be grateful if you would report this to us. By doing so, you can save other readers from frustration and help us improve subsequent versions of this book. If you find any errata, please report them by visiting http://www.packtpub.com/submit-errata, selecting your book, clicking on the **errata submission form** link, and entering the details of your errata. Once your errata are verified, your submission will be accepted and the errata will be uploaded on our website, or added to any list of existing errata, under the Errata section of that title. Any existing errata can be viewed by selecting your title from http://www.packtpub.com/support.

Piracy

Piracy of copyright material on the Internet is an ongoing problem across all media. At Packt, we take the protection of our copyright and licenses very seriously. If you come across any illegal copies of our works, in any form, on the Internet, please provide us with the location address or website name immediately so that we can pursue a remedy.

Please contact us at copyright@packtpub.com with a link to the suspected pirated material.

We appreciate your help in protecting our authors, and our ability to bring you valuable content.

Questions

You can contact us at questions@packtpub.com if you are having a problem with any aspect of the book, and we will do our best to address it.

1
Installing and Setting Up Xamarin Studio

Software developers are very selective with the tools they work with. We take the time to evaluate our goals and examine our available options. Then, we compare these options to our goals to determine the best tool for the task at hand. Xamarin Studio is one tool we can choose for cross-platform development using .NET. It is not a one-size-fits-all solution for all of your development needs. Instead, it's a specialized tool that allows .NET developers to efficiently create applications that can run on multiple platforms while using the technologies they are already familiar and experienced with.

The purpose of this chapter is to help you install and set up Xamarin Studio, as well as the ancillary tools you will need to effectively develop in a cross-platform environment.

In this chapter, we will cover the following topics:

- Xamarin Studio pricing plans
- Xamarin Studio platform options
- Installing Xcode and the iOS SDK
- Installing Xamarin Studio
- Apple Developer Program
- Google Play Developer Program
- Installing simulators and emulators
- Improving AVD performance
- Setting up test devices
- Setting up source control
- Additional resources for cross-platform developers

Xamarin Studio pricing plans

As of June 2014, Xamarin offers four subscription plans for developers to choose from: **Starter**, **Indie**, **Business**, and **Enterprise**. The details and prices of these plans presented here are accurate as of the time this was written, but be aware that they are subject to change.

Starter

At the entry level, Xamarin offers the Starter edition of Xamarin Studio. In many respects, this edition is similar to a fully functional trial except that there is no expiration date on the license. This edition is perfectly suitable to demonstrate the guides and walkthroughs presented in this text. At this point, you might ask yourself why you would need to actually spend money and enroll in one of the professional editions. For most people, the reason is that the Starter edition is limited in three very important aspects.

First, this edition limits the size of your compiled packages to 64 KB. This is so limited even some of the demonstration apps bundled with the Xamarin Studio installation are too large to be run. Secondly, the Starter edition does not allow development from within Visual Studio. Finally, this edition does not offer access to downloadable components and permits calls to third-party native libraries. For example, while developing a simple Android application using the Starter edition, I wanted to implement the `IParcelable` interface, only to learn that my subscription did not permit me to include the necessary module. I promptly upgraded my plan. Well played, Xamarin.

Indie

Next up is the Indie edition. Similar to the Starter edition, Indie is fully functional. However, with the Indie edition you are permitted to call out to third-party native libraries. More importantly, your compiled application size is no longer limited to 64 KB, and it can effectively be as large as your target device can handle. Without this limitation, Indie also permits building apps using the Xamarin.Forms framework introduced in Xamarin 3. Although the Indie edition does not allow `System.Data.SqlClient` to be referenced in your project, you may still integrate other third-party components such as sqlite-netORM to provide data store functionality.

It's worth pointing out that, similar to the Starter edition, Indie does not allow you to develop within Visual Studio. If developing directly in Visual Studio is a critical requirement for your process, then the Indie edition isn't for you. However, all of the independent Xamarin developers that I am acquainted with, myself included, use this edition and they are satisfied.

Business

Cited as being the most popular option, the Xamarin Business edition offers everything that the Indie edition offered, plus several additional features. First, you can develop, deploy, and debug from within Visual Studio. Secondly, you have access to private e-mail support from Xamarin. Finally, and arguably most importantly, this plan has support for in-house deployment, headless builds, WCF, and `System.Data.SqlClient`. Code troubleshooting assistance from Xamarin experts is also available with this edition at an additional cost.

Note that if you are a company or an incorporated entity with five or more employees, you may not purchase the Indie edition but must purchase the Business or Enterprise editions instead.

Enterprise

Finally, the Enterprise edition offers some additional perks in the form of supplementary support options, bundled prime components, access to Hotfixes, and a dedicated Technical Account Manager. This plan is topped off by a guaranteed one-day response service-level agreement, which can be a valuable asset when your team is facing a tough challenge under a tight deadline.

Understanding the pricing structure

Xamarin editions are not based on licensing the development studio itself, but rather on the platform the developer will be working with. This means if you or your team wants to develop iPhone apps, you will need to purchase one of the plans for the iOS platform. This license will permit you to develop any type of iOS app from iPhones to iPads or iPod Touch, but it will not permit you to develop applications for Android devices. In order to develop in both iOS and Android, you will need to purchase two plans. This is also true for the Mac platform.

These plans are subscriptions that must be renewed annually. If you decide not to renew the subscription, Xamarin Studio will continue to function and you will still have access to your development platform and your work. However, you will no longer have access to new releases or ongoing support.

Additionally, Xamarin offers special discounts to various groups. To inquire about the specifics of these offers, you will need to contact Xamarin sales directly:

- Open source projects that plan to contribute to the Xamarin framework can receive complimentary non-commercial licenses for Xamarin products.
- MSDN subscribers can get a 30 percent to 50 percent discount for their annual subscription costs.

- Businesses purchasing a large number of licenses can receive a volume discount.
- Start-ups less than 3 years old and small businesses with fewer than 20 employees can get special discounts as well.
- Finally, the academic discount applies to professors teaching courses on Xamarin and any students enrolled in accredited institutions. This discount allows eligible developers to purchase a Business edition (without e-mail support) of Xamarin.iOS, Xamarin.Android, and/or Xamarin.Mac for $99.

An example company

As an example, let's assume a company has 14 employees, seven of whom are developers, and this company is endeavoring to create a cross-platform mobile application. One developer will be focusing on writing the shared logic using Visual Studio, two will be developing the Windows Phone UI, another two will develop the Android UI, and the remaining two will develop the iPhone UI. Three of these developers will not need a Xamarin license, while two will require an iOS platform license and two will require an Android platform license. Since this company has more than five employees, only the Business and Enterprise plans are acceptable. Therefore, at a minimum, this company must procure four business plan subscriptions at an annual cost of roughly $4,000.

This may seem like a steep price for a small company to absorb, but it's really quite cost effective. If you compare this subscription cost to the cost of merely recruiting four full-time specialist developers, you will immediately see the advantage that Xamarin Studio provides to your organization.

 Do you need more information? For more specific details on the pricing plans, see the *Pricing* section of Xamarin's FAQ at `http://www.xamarin.com/faq`.

Xamarin Studio platform options

Xamarin Studio enables .NET developers to build applications that target three distinct platforms: Android, iOS, and Mac. Xamarin Studio is the Core Integrated Development Environment and is required for development on any of these target platforms. In addition to Xamarin Studio, you will need to install the specific plugin for your target platform. These plugins are detailed in the following sections.

Xamarin.Android

The **Xamarin.Android** package is required to develop applications that target the Android platform. Android development with Xamarin can be performed on any Windows PC or Mac that meets the minimum system requirements. The **Android SDK** is required for development, and it will be downloaded during the Xamarin Studio installation.

Xamarin.iOS

Xamarin.iOS is required to develop applications that target the iOS platform. The iOS development with Xamarin can be performed on any Windows PC or Mac that meets the minimum system requirements. However, in order to develop on a Windows PC a networked Mac is required as a build and deployment machine. **Xcode** and the **iOS SDK** are also required for development, and they must be installed prior to installing Xamarin.iOS. Additionally, at the time of writing this Xamarin Studio is unable to generate a proxy file for WCF services. Therefore, if you intend to utilize the WCF services in your iOS application, you will need a Windows machine to generate the proxy files.

Xamarin.Mac

Xamarin.Mac is required to develop applications that target the Mac platform. At the time of writing this, Mac development with Xamarin can only be performed on a Mac running at Lion (OS X 10.7) or higher, which meets the minimum system requirements. Xcode is also required for development, and it must be installed prior to installing Xamarin.Mac.

Installing development components

Before we begin installing Xamarin Studio and the necessary supporting components, it's important to note that this book's perspective is developing iOS, Android, and Mac applications on a Mac. This means that the names and conventions will be those you'll see when working with Mac OS X. In most cases, the differences between a Mac OS X environment and a Windows environment will be negligible and, therefore, I won't discuss them. However, in the cases where the differences are significant, or where there is a different process to be followed, the details will be pointed out and highlighted. In some cases, entire portions of the book (such as the *Installing the Visual Studio plugin* section in *Chapter 4*, *Plugins, Templates, Libraries, and Files*) will be dedicated to the Windows platform environment.

Installing Xcode and the iOS SDK

Xcode is Apple's premier (and free for all OS X users) integrated development environment to develop Mac, iPad, iPhone, and iPod Touch applications. Additionally, the iOS SDK comes bundled with Xcode upon installation. Since the Xcode application's release cycle closely matches that of the Mac and iOS platforms, you as a developer can expect to always have access to the tools needed to develop applications that target the latest iOS platforms.

Although Xamarin Studio 5 comes bundled with its own interface builder, this tool only supports storyboard development as of the time this was written. Xcode provides an interface builder to create graphical user interfaces for iOS and Mac development using storyboards as well as XIB files. Also, the package includes **Instruments**, which is a graphical user interface tool for application performance analysis and visualization. We will discuss Instruments more in *Chapter 7, Testing and Debugging*.

> If you do not intend to develop iOS applications, you may skip this section for now and come back to it whenever you're ready. However, you will not be able to install Xamarin.iOS or Xamarin.Mac until Xcode and the iOS SDK have been installed.

Installing Xcode from the App Store

To install Xcode, perform the following steps:

1. Open the App Store from the Dock or Finder.
2. If you have not already done so, log in by navigating to **Store** | **Log In** and entering your credentials.
3. If you are visiting the App Store for the first time, you will need to create an account. For details on creating an App Store account, see the Apple support documentation at http://support.apple.com/kb/HT4479.
4. In the spotlight, type xcode and begin the search.

5. Select the **Xcode Developer Tools** app and then click the **Install App** button. This will begin the download and initial installation process, as shown in the following screenshot:

Xcode is not a simple application, and the initial download is just over 2 GB in size. Therefore, depending on your connection speed, you may need to wait for some time. If you get bored and want to see how things are progressing, hover over launchpad in the Dock and you will see the current download/installation progress. Alternatively, you can open launchpad and view the progress there as well.

Installing Xcode manually

On the other hand, if you don't have an App Store account or for some reason you don't want to use one for this purpose, you can also download the Xcode installer manually from `https://developer.apple.com/xcode/`.

Perform the following steps to download Xcode manually:

1. When you arrive at the download page, you will see the **Download Xcode 5 for free.** section as shown in the preceding screenshot.
2. Click the **View downloads** link.

3. When you reach the program list, type `xcode 5` in the search field and hit *Enter*.
4. Your search results should include the latest Xcode 5 installer, as shown in the following screenshot:

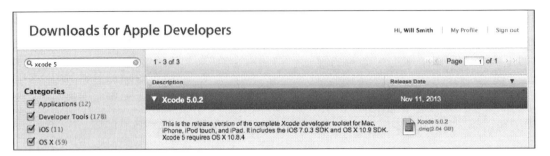

5. Click the download link to the right-hand side of the product description.
6. Once the download is complete, open the file and continue.
7. Follow the prompts.

Finishing the Xcode installation

Once the download has completed, we will still need to open Xcode from the launcher to begin to finalize the installation. The steps are as follows:

1. Open the launcher.
2. Open Xcode.
3. Accept **Xcode and iOS SDK License Agreement**.
4. When prompted, enter your system credentials to give the installer permission to continue.

Installing Xamarin Studio

Once Xcode has finished installing, the only prerequisite you have is the Xamarin Studio Unified Installer, which could not install on its own. All of the other prerequisites for cross-platform development, such as the Java SDK, the Android SDK, and the Mono Framework, will be installed concurrently with Xamarin Studio as needed based on the products you choose. Let's begin installing Xamarin Studio:

1. First, we need to download the Xamarin unified installer from http://www.xamarin.com/download.

Chapter 1

> If you haven't purchased a subscription yet, or if you simply want to download the Starter edition, you can just *tell them about yourself* and click **Download Xamarin** for your platform. However, if you have created an account or you have already purchased a subscription, you will need to click **Sign In** on this page and follow the link to download Xamarin Studio on the landing page that follows.

2. If you are trying out Starter edition anonymously, your download should begin automatically. If you have logged in, you will need to click **Download** under your highlighted current plan.
3. Once the Xamarin Studio Unified Installer finishes downloading, you need to run the installer.
4. When the splash screen appears, double click on the **Install Xamarin.app** icon.
5. When the installer opens, you will need to review the Xamarin software license. If you agree to the terms, click the **Accept** button to proceed.
6. Next, you need to select the plugins you want to install. In my case, I selected all three, as shown in the following screenshot. However, you should choose the plugins you intend to work with.

[15]

Installing and Setting Up Xamarin Studio

7. If you chose to install **Xamarin.Android** on the next screen, you will be asked to configure the installation to specify where the Android SDK will be installed, as shown in the following screenshot:

8. After reviewing the prerequisites that need to be installed, take a moment to review the additional licenses as they are presented. If you agree to the terms, click **Accept** to proceed.

9. Once you have accepted the last batch of licenses, you have an opportunity to take a short break while the installation proceeds. As you can see from the following screenshot, Xamarin Studio is another large application:

> While the Xcode installation was self-sufficient after it was set in motion, the Xamarin Studio installation may require you provide your system credentials for some of the components being installed. So once the installation starts, you can go ahead and take that break you've been looking forward to. However, just be sure to check in on your machine from time to time.

10. Once the installation is complete, please take a moment to review the progress report before closing the installer.

> If your installation experiences any common errors or some components fail to install completely, just restart the installer. Those components successfully downloaded and installed will persist, and the installer won't try to download them again. For example, during my first attempt Xamarin.iOS failed to download. I restarted the installer and after a few minutes, the component was up and running.

You have now installed the most basic tools you need for developing in Xamarin Studio. Now, let's begin by exploring the various **Apple Developer Programs** and the **Google Play Developer Program**.

> Having developed and maintained applications for both iOS and Android devices, I learned that the two platforms are very different—not only in terms of functionality, but also in development process. If you are new to developing for mobile devices in general, I suggest that you choose one platform to focus on and work through that development track for the remainder of this text. Then, once you are comfortable developing for that platform, come back and work through the opposing platform.
>
> Furthermore, it is my opinion that iOS is the easiest platform to learn for a first-time Xamarin user. Nevertheless, please make your decision based on your specific goals.

Apple Developer Program

It's not technically necessary to have an Apple Developer Program account to develop iOS or Mac applications. However, you will need to have one if you intend to release your app to the App Store. Additionally, you won't be able to test your application on your own personal mobile devices without an active account, specifically an **iOS Developer Program** account. This may seem unfair at first, but keep in mind that an active account enables you to create a provisioning profile for your application. A provisioning profile is a certificate that lets your device know that your application comes from a trusted source and is permissible to execute. We will discuss provisioning profiles in more detail later in this chapter.

As stated, the iOS Developer Program account lets you deploy applications to your iOS devices for testing and to the App Store for sale once the application has passed Apple's QA process. Apple also offers the **Mac Developer Program** to develop Mac applications. Again, you can develop Mac apps using Xamarin Studio without holding a Mac Developer Program account. The difference is that you can test your application on your physical machine without holding an active account. You will only need an active Mac Developer Program account if you intend to release your app to the App Store.

Each of the developer program accounts carries an annual subscription cost of $99, whether you are an individual developer or a business entity with multiple developers. Under both programs, Apple will also collect 30 percent of every App Store sale. The iOS Developer Program also has an Enterprise class for businesses planning to develop apps exclusively for in-house purposes. This subscription costs $299 per year, presumably because these apps will not produce any revenue for Apple through sales in the App Store.

Why don't I just jailbreak my device?

While I've heard rumors that it is possible to jailbreak your mobile device to enable deployment testing without having an active iOS Developer Program account, what would be the point?

The security you are removing is there to protect your equipment. More importantly, you will still need to get an account at some point before you can distribute your application to paying customers. Without an account, you won't even be able to easily distribute your application to testers or a contract customer using **TestFlight**. In my opinion, $99 a year is a small price to pay to maintain your integrity and professional reputation.

The steps required to subscribe to either the iOS or the Mac Developer Programs are the same. Also, the only difference between subscribing as an individual versus a business entity is that a business will require a free **D&B D-U-N-S Number**. D-U-N-S Numbers are a unique nine-digit identifier for businesses issued by Dun & Bradstreet. This identifier has become the standard to track businesses worldwide. Many businesses, including most of the Fortune 500 companies, require a D-U-N-S Number when you are applying to do business with them as a supplier, contractor, or consultant. If your business does not currently have a D-U-N-S Number, you will have an opportunity to obtain one prior to creating your developer program account.

Be aware that the process of obtaining a D-U-N-S Number is not automated, and it may take several business days to finalize once you have completed and submitted the brief application.

Let's walk through the process of subscribing to an iOS Developer Program account now.

If you do not intend to develop iOS applications, you may skip this walkthrough for now and come back to it whenever you're ready.

Perform the following steps to subscribe to an iOS Developer Program account:

1. Open your browser and go to `https://developer.apple.com/programs/`.
2. Click on the **iOS Developer Program** section.
3. Click the **Enroll Now** button.
4. Click the **Continue** button.
5. You will have the option to enroll with your current Apple ID or create a new ID for this purpose. For this demonstration, we will assume you are using your current ID. Click the **Continue** button next to your current ID.
6. Decide whether you are enrolling as an **Individual** or as a **Company** and click the appropriate button.
7. For whichever plan you choose, fill out the required information and click the **Continue** button.
8. Choose the programs you wish to subscribe to and click the **Continue** button.
9. Review your information and click the **Continue** button.
10. Review any terms and conditions presented. If you agree to the terms check the boxes and click the **I Agree** button.
11. Review your shopping cart and click the **Buy Now** button.
12. Activate your new account.

Google Play Developer Program

Google offers a developer program for Android devices called the Google Play Developer Program. Like the Apple programs, it is not necessary to have a Google Play Developer Program account to develop Android applications. Unlike the iOS program, you can deploy to your personal devices without an active Google Play Developer Program account. You will only need a Google Play Developer account if you intend to sell your app on the Google Play Store. At the time of writing this, Google charges a one-time fee of $25 for a developer program account for an individual or a business.

> If you do not intend to develop Android applications, you may skip this walkthrough for now and come back to it whenever you're ready.

Let's walk through the process of subscribing to a Google Play Developer Program account now:

1. Open your browser and go to `https://play.google.com/apps/publish/signup/`.
2. Sign in with your Google account and click the **Continue** button.
3. Review the **Google Play Developer distribution agreement**. If you agree to the terms select the checkbox and click the **Continue to payment** button.
4. Enter your payment information and click **Accept and continue**.
5. Once your payment has been accepted, you will need to create your Developer Profile. Enter your name, e-mail address, website (if applicable), and phone number and click the **Complete registration** button.

Once you have completed the registration, you will be redirected to the Google Play **Developer Console**. We will discuss the Developer Console in more detail in *Chapter 8, Deployment*.

Setting up simulators and emulators

Technically speaking, simulators and emulators are different technologies. Within the context of our discussions on mobile application testing, it is important to note that Android testing is performed on an emulator, while iOS testing is performed on a simulator. At first this may seem like pure semantics, but in fact it is a very critical distinction for a mobile developer to understand.

Android emulators attempt to emulate the characteristics and environment found on an actual device. This means if your device has 2 GB of RAM, then the emulator will likewise be limited to 2 GB of RAM, hence the term emulator. An iOS simulator, on the other hand, has access to your full system resources. This means that if your Mac has a 32 GB RAM with a 2.3 GHz i7 quad-core processors, so does that iPhone simulator you're testing on, even though a true iPhone device does not have 32 GB of RAM or an i7 processor. Do you see the potential problems presented by this design?

No matter how intense your application is, or how much processing power it requires, there will almost always be an ample supply of resources available to the simulator. Inside the simulator, your application will be lightning fast and, unless you have a leak somewhere in your code, it will probably never run into memory issues. This is not a real-world testing environment, which is why the iOS testing environment is referred to as a simulator.

Beyond these differences, at least for the purpose of our discussions of virtual mobile application testing, let's just assume that the remaining differences truly are semantic. Additionally, the Android SDK refers to an emulator as an **Android Virtual Device (AVD)**. So, in the further chapters of this book, when we are testing iOS applications in a virtual environment, we are using a simulator. Also, when we are testing Android applications in a virtual environment, we are using an emulator or AVD.

iOS simulators

Luckily for us, the latest iOS simulators come bundled with Xcode and require very little, if any, setup before they can be used. This means you can test iOS 7 simulators for iPhone, iPhone, iPad, and iPad Mini devices right out of the box. However, if you want to make your apps backward compatible with an iOS 6 device, which is an entirely reasonable expectation, you will still need to download the iOS 6.1Simulator package.

To install the iOS 6.1 Simulator, perform the following steps:

1. Open Xcode.
2. Navigate to **Xcode | Preferences**.
3. Select the **Downloads** tab and you will see the following window:

4. In the **Components** group, click the arrow to the right of **iOS 6.1 Simulator**.
5. Once the download is complete, the new simulators will be available inside Xamarin Studio.

Android emulators

Ideally, setting up an AVD for various Android devices should be simple. As is often the case in development, ideal conditions are not the norm. Since there are so many types of devices and configurations that can run the Android OS, it is not feasible to simply include boxed AVDs for every one of them. As you are about to see, the file sizes associated with even one boxed AVD image makes the idea of simply including them all with the installation of the SDK impossible to implement. Therefore, it is typically left up to the developer to create an AVD definition and image to match the target platform. Although a detailed walkthrough of every permutation of Android version and device configuration is beyond the scope of this book, let's look at setting up an AVD for the popular Nexus 7 tablet as well as the Samsung Galaxy S4 as typical examples.

Creating a Nexus 7 AVD using the AVD Manager

We'll start by creating a user-defined Nexus 7 image. In the case of the Nexus 7, there is a basic image prepackaged with the SDK installation. Assuming we want to create a Nexus 7 image with a different configuration for our testing, we can use this packaged image as a starting point for creating our own. We will accomplish this by **cloning** the existing image.

To create a Nexus 7 user image through cloning, perform the following steps:

1. Inside Xamarin Studio, navigate to **Tools** | **Open AVD Manager**.
2. Select the **Device Definitions** tab.
3. Select the **Nexus 7 by Google** image.
4. Click **Create AVD**.
5. Change the **AVD Name** field by entering name for the AVD.
6. Leave the **Device** value as default.
7. From the **Target** drop-down list, select **Android 4.4.2 – API Level 19**. Your dialog should resemble the following screenshot:

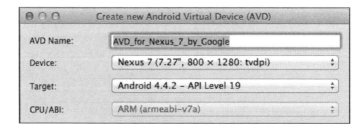

8. Leave all of the other settings at their default values and click the **OK** button.

Once the new user image has been created, it will be available for use during testing with Xamarin Studio.

Creating a Samsung Galaxy S4 AVD using the SDK and AVD Manager

Now, let's create a custom user image. For this walkthrough, we'll create a Samsung Galaxy S4 AVD. This device emulator is not bundled with the SDK, and in fact, it requires an additional SDK from Sony in order to be created.

To create a Samsung Galaxy S4 AVD, perform the following steps:

1. Inside Xamarin Studio, go to **Tools | Open SDK Manager**.
2. Once the **SDK Manager** opens, go to **Tools | Manage Add-On Sites**.
3. Select the **User Defined Sites** tab.
4. Click **New**.
5. Enter `http://dl-developer.sonymobile.com/sdk_manager/Sony-Add-on-SDK.xml` in the field provided and click **OK**.
6. Close the **Add-on Sites** dialog.
7. Check whether the **Sort by** property at the bottom of the dialog window is set to **API Level**.
8. Expand the **Android 4.1.2 (API 16)** group.
9. Select the checkbox for **Sony Add-on SDK**.
10. Scroll down and expand the **Extras** group.
11. Select the checkbox for **Sony Device Profiles**.
12. Click **Install 2 packages**.
13. Once these packages are installed, you may close the **SDK Manager**.
14. Inside Xamarin Studio, navigate to **Tools | Open AVD Manager**.
15. Select the **Device Definitions** tab.
16. Select the **XPeria Z1** image.
17. Click **Clone**.
18. Insert `Samsung Galaxy S4` in the **Name** field.

Installing and Setting Up Xamarin Studio

19. Set the **Buttons** value to **Hardware** and your dialog should resemble the following screenshot:

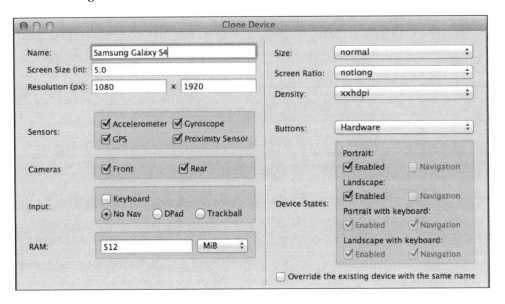

20. Click **Clone Device**.
21. If the settings were accepted, the **Clone Device** dialog should close and you will be back at the **AVD Manager**. Return to the **Android Virtual Devices** tab.
22. Click **New**.
23. In the **AVD Name** field, enter a name for your AVD, for example, `GalaxyS4_1`.
24. From the **Device** drop-down list, select the definition you just created. In my case, the definition is named **Samsung Galaxy S4 (1080 x 1920: xxhdpi)**.
25. From the **Target** drop-down list, select **Sony Add-on SDK 2.1 (Sony) – API Level 16**.
26. For the **Front Camera** and **Back Camera** lists, choose how you would like to emulate the cameras. Your options are to not emulate them at all (**None**), emulate them through software (**Emulated**), or to use a webcam (**Web Camera**).

27. Under the **Emulation Options** group, select the checkbox for **Use Host GPU**. Your dialog should resemble the following screenshot:

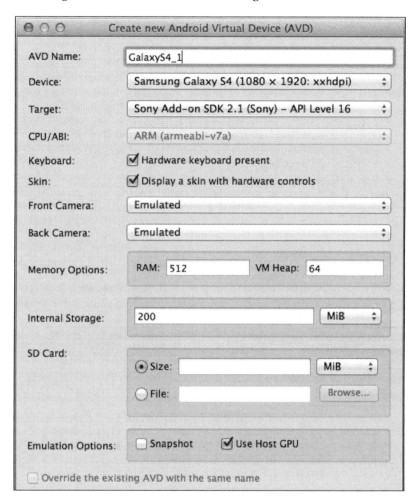

28. Leave all the remaining settings at their default values and click **OK**.
29. Review the various licenses that are presented. If you agree to the terms of each, click the **Accept Licenses** button.

Once the new user image has been created, it will be available for use during testing with Xamarin Studio.

Improving AVD performance

Once you've had the opportunity to work with one of the AVDs, you will notice right away that they are very sluggish during their initial startup, and only marginally faster on subsequent startups. This behavior is consistent on both Mac and Windows machines running Intel chipsets, but it seems to be especially true on Windows. However, don't be discouraged by this initial performance because there are steps that can be taken to significantly improve this.

> All of the performance measurements cited in this section are averages based on tests performed on my personal development machine. For example, I tested my user-defined Nexus 7 AVD and clocked an average initial start up time of just over 3 minutes, and an average subsequent start up time of just over 2 minutes. These average measurements will serve as the benchmarks for later testing and comparison.

Intel x86 Atom System Image

Most Android devices run ARM processors. Likewise, the out-of-the-box AVDs are based on the ARM system image called the **APM EABI v7a System Image**. Although the ARM processor architecture is highly efficient and suitable for mobile device applications, it is also quite different from Intel architecture. As a result, the ARM system image performs very poorly when emulated on an Intel chipset.

Intel is aware of this performance issue and has responded by creating its own system image called **Intel x86 Atom System Image**. This image was designed for the specific purpose of running AVDs on Intel-based machines, and it can significantly improve AVD startup and operational performance. The only drawback is Intel x86 Atom is not available for every target API level at this time.

Let's create a new AVD from scratch, but this time target the Intel x86 Atom System Image:

1. Inside Xamarin Studio, go to **Tools | Open SDK Manager**.
2. Once the **SDK Manager** opens, go to **Tools | Manage Add-On Sites**.
3. Select the **User Defined Sites** tab.
4. Confirm that the **Android x86 System Image** property exists.
    - If not, click the **New** button
    - Enter `https://dl-ssl.google.com/android/repository/sys-img/x86/sys-img.xml` and click **OK**
5. Close the **Add-on Sites** dialog.

6. Confirm that the **Sort by** property at the bottom of the dialog window is set to **API Level**.
7. Scroll down and expand the **Android 4.4.2 (API 19)** group.
8. Select the **Intel x86 Atom System Image** checkbox.
9. Click **Install 1 package**.
10. Once this package is installed, you may close the **SDK Manager**.
11. Inside Xamarin Studio, go to **Tools | Open AVD Manager**.
12. Select the **Device Definitions** tab.
13. Select the **Nexus 7 by Google** image.
14. Click the **Create AVD** button.
15. In the **AVD Name** field, type AVD_for_Nexus_7_by_Google.
16. From the **Target** drop-down list, select **Android 4.4.2 – API Level 19**.
17. From the **CPU/ABI** drop-down list, select **Intel Atom (x86)**. Now, your dialog should resemble the following screenshot:

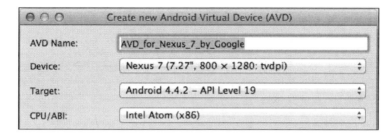

18. Leave all of the other settings at their default values and click **OK**.

Try using your new Nexus 7 AVD and compare the speed to that of the original, ARM-based AVD. You should see a marked improvement in both startup and operational performance.

Hardware Acceleration Execution Manager

So, you've tried out your new Nexus 7 AVD running on the Inter x86 Atom image. Now you're thinking, "This is good, but can it be better?". To coin a phrase, "Gentlemen, we can rebuild it. We have the technology."

Installing and Setting Up Xamarin Studio

If you are running a fairly up-to-date computer with an Intel chip that has **Intel® Virtualization Technology** enabled, you can utilize the **Intel Hardware Acceleration Execution Manager (HAXM)**. HAXM is capable of easily improving performance by an order of magnitude. Coupled with an AVD built on the Intel x86 Atom system image, the improvement is almost astounding.

> Note that there is a specific hardware prerequisite to use this technology. Your machine, whether it is Mac OS or Windows, must have an Intel processor with support for Intel VT-x, EM64T and **Execute Disable (XD)** Bit functionality enabled in **Basic Input/Output System (BIOS)**.

AXM can be installed in three steps. First, you need to make sure that virtualization technology is enabled in the BIOS. Then, you need to install the HAXM add-on through the **SDK Manager**. Finally, you need to run the executable for your system.

Since virtualization technology is typically turned on by default on most systems, we'll start by installing the HAXM add-on through the **SDK Manager** by using the following steps:

1. Inside Xamarin Studio, go to **Tools | Open SDK Manager**.
2. Once **SDK Manager** opens, go to **Tools | Manage Add-On Sites**.
3. Select the **User Defined Sites** tab.
4. Confirm that the **Intel HAXM** property exists.
   - If not, click the **New** button
   - Enter `https://dl-ssl.google.com/android/repository/extras/intel/addon.xml` and click **OK**
5. Close the **Add-on Sites** dialog.
6. Confirm that the **Sort by** property at the bottom of the dialog window is set to **API Level**.
7. Scroll down and expand the **Extras** group.
8. Select the **Intel x86 Emulator Accelerator (HAXM)** checkbox.
9. Click **Install 1 package**.
10. Once this package is installed, you can close the **SDK Manager**.

> You may have noticed that the HAXM entry in **SDK Manager** was listed as **Installed** when you were finished. This is just poor design on the part of the **SDK Manager**, in my opinion, because the package is not fully installed quite yet. To do this, we need to launch the HAXM executable.

Chapter 1

11. Open **Finder** (or **Explorer** in Windows) and navigate to `<sdk>/extras/intel/Hardware_Accelerated_Execution_Manager/`.

12. From here, launch `IntelHAXM.dmg` (`IntelHAXM.exe` in Windows).

13. Proceed through the HAXM installation process. When you reach the screen titled **Memory Limit for Intel HAXM**, it's best to just leave the default setting for now as you can go back and change it later if necessary. Setting this value too high initially can cause poor performance in other applications on your system while the HAXM is running.

> If during the installation you receive an error message stating that Intel® Virtualization Technology is not turned on, you will need to enable it in BIOS before you can proceed. Enter your system's BIOS settings, set **Virtualization Technology: [Enabled]**, and then restart the executable.

At this stage, you should be enjoying much faster performance of your AVDs. In fact, HAXM can make those AVDs based on the Intel x86 Atom image run at near native speeds! Initial startup of the AVD takes around 25 seconds on my machine, while subsequent startups take around 17 seconds. There's still one more item we can tweak in our AVD setup to squeeze out just a little more startup performance.

Run from Snapshot

If you edit one of your AVD definitions, at the bottom you will see a group titled **Emulation Options**. Within that group there are two options that improve performance, **Snapshot** and **Use Host GPU**. One improves start up performance and the other improves general operating performance. Unfortunately, you can only use one of these improvements at a time. For the sake of our discussion, let's assume we are more concerned with faster start up times, so we will set the option to **Snapshot**:

1. Inside Xamarin Studio, go to **Tools | Open AVD Manager**.
2. Select the **Device Definitions** tab.
3. Select the **Nexus 7 by Google** image.
4. Click **Create AVD**.
5. Change the **AVD Name** field.
6. From the **Target** drop-down list, select **Android 4.4.2 – API Level 19**.
7. From the **CPU/ABI** drop-down list, select **Intel Atom (x86)**.

8. In the **Emulation Options** group, select **Snapshot** as shown in the following screenshot:

9. Leave all of the other settings at their default values and click **OK**.

This new AVD is based on the Intel x86 Atom system image and is set to run from **Snapshot**. As long as HAXM is running on our system, your initial start up time will still be about the same, but subsequent startups should clock in much faster. On my development machine, start up time still averaged about 25 seconds, but subsequent start up times averaged 5 seconds! Now when your fellow developers tell you that the AVDs running on the packaged SDK are painfully sluggish, you'll know they just haven't applied themselves to finding a solution to the problem.

Third-party AVD options

Do you still feel the need for more speed? No worries, I won't judge. At this stage, if you want to improve performance even further, you need to start looking at alternatives to the SDK Emulator platform. There are several third-party packages that provide comparable and, in some cases, even better performance over the SDK emulators. **GenyMotion** is one popular alternative that is currently available for free to individual developers and small companies. GenyMotion provides an alternative to the entire emulator paradigm, replacing emulation with virtualization. I personally use the GenyMotion Free edition and I have been very pleased with its performance.

> GenyMotion, as well as any other alternative to AVD emulation, is not essential software for working in Xamarin Studio. Therefore, installing and setting up the software is beyond the scope of this book. However, if you are interested in trying out GenyMotion, you can download and try out the free version at `https://shop.genymotion.com/index.php? controller=order-opc`.

Setting up test devices

Simulators and AVDs are acceptable for development testing, but it is unwise to rely solely on these virtual environments. Therefore, it is important to test on at least one physical device that matches your target environment.

Setting up iOS devices

Although setting up the iOS simulator is a joy, setting up devices for testing is anything but a joy. To test using your iOS device, you must have several items in place. If you have been following along up until now, you already have your Apple iOS Developer Program account. Now, you need a development certificate and a provisioning profile for your device.

> If you do not intend to develop iOS applications, you may skip this walkthrough for now and come back to it whenever you're ready.

Obtaining a development certificate

There are two ways to generate your development certificate, and the method you choose is largely based on whether you are developing on a Mac or on a Windows machine. First, for those who are developing on a Mac, we'll look at how to generate your development certificate and associate it with your application within Xamarin Studio. Here are the steps you need to follow:

1. Open your solution inside Xamarin Studio.
2. Go to **Xamarin Studio** | **Preferences**.
3. Under the **Environment** group, select the **Developer Accounts** panel.
4. Click the plus (+) button.
5. Enter your Apple ID and password in the dialog that appears.
6. Your credentials will be verified and Xamarin will automatically generate the developer certificate for that account.
7. Close the **Preferences** dialog.
8. Double-click on the start-up project, which will open the **Project Options** dialog.
9. In the **Build** group, choose the **iOS Application** item.
10. Open the **Team** drop-down list and choose your developer account.
11. Click **OK**.

For those developing iOS applications on a Windows machine, the process is only slightly more involved and requires manual generation of the developer certificate. The steps are follows:

1. On your Mac, open **Finder**.
2. Open **Keychain Access** by navigating to **Applications** | **Utilities**.

3. Open **Keychain Access | Certificate Assistant | Request a Certificate From a Certificate Authority**.
4. Enter your e-mail address and name.
5. Under the **Request** group, choose **Saved to disk**.
6. Click the **Continue** button.
7. When prompted, save the file on your desktop.
8. Open a browser and log in to the **Certificates, Identifiers, and Profiles** section of the **Developer Portal** at `https://developer.apple.com/account/overview.action`.
9. In the **Certificates** section, choose the **iOS Apps** column.
10. Click the plus (+) button to create a new certificate.
11. For the type of certificate, choose **iOS App Development**.
12. Click **Continue**.
13. On the **Generate your certificate** screen, upload the certificate file you saved previously.
14. Click **Generate**.
15. Download your new certificate.
16. Open the file. This will add the certificate to Keychain.

Provisioning your devices

Now that you have a developer certificate for your applications to link to, you still need to add your devices to your developer account by a process called provisioning. To provision a device, we must first create a provisioning profile containing that device's information. You must repeat the following process for every device you want to provision. Here are the steps you need to follow:

1. Plug your device into your Mac and launch iTunes.
2. From the sidebar select your device.
3. Click on the **Serial Number** value.
4. The serial number will change to **Identifier (UDID)**.
5. Copy the serial number value.
6. Open a browser and log in to the **Certificates, Identifiers, and Profiles** section of the **Developer Portal** at `https://developers.apple.com/account/overview.action`.
7. Open the **Devices** section and click the plus (+) button.

8. Enter a name for your device and the UDID you copied from iTunes.
9. Click **Continue**.
10. Verify that your new information is included in the list of devices and that it is correct.
11. Click **Submit.**
12. Once the profile is generated, click **Download**.
13. Open iTunes again and select your device.
14. Drag the provisioning profile file to the **Library** in iTunes.
15. Click the **Sync** button, and the profile will be installed to your device.

Setting up Android devices

In order to test on an Android device, three steps must be performed:

1. First, you must enable debugging on the device.
2. Next, you may need to install additional USB drivers.
3. Finally, you need to connect your device to your computer using a USB or alternately via Wi-Fi.

> If you do not intend to develop Android applications, you may skip this walkthrough for now and come back to it whenever you're ready.

Enabling debugging on your device

To enable debugging on Android 3.2 and older devices, perform the following steps:

1. On your device, open the **Application** menu.
2. Go to **Settings**.
3. Select **Applications**.
4. Select the **Development** item.
5. Check **USB Debugging**.

To enable debugging on Android 4.0 to 4.1, perform the following steps:

1. On your device, go to the **Settings** screen.
2. Select **Developer Options**.
3. Uncheck the **USB Debugging** option.

To enable debugging on Android 4.2 and higher, perform the following steps:

1. On your device, go to the **Settings** screen.
2. Open the **About Phone** group.
3. Tap the **Build Number** item seven times (yes, I'm serious).
4. Go back to the **Settings** screen.
5. Select **Applications**.
6. Select the **Development** item.
7. Check **USB Debugging**.

Installing USB drivers and connecting your device

Using a USB cable is the easiest method of connecting your device and development machine. If you are developing on a Mac, you just need to plug it in. If you are developing on a Windows machine, you may also need to install additional USB drivers for your specific device. Since each manufacturer tends to release their own unique USB drivers, you will need to search over the Internet for the specific instructions for your device.

Under certain circumstances, however, you may want to use Wi-Fi to connect to your device. Connecting via Wi-Fi is completely optional so you may skip this section if it doesn't apply to you. Perform the following steps:

1. Ensure that your device is connected to the same Wi-Fi network as your development machine.
2. On your device, go to **Settings** | **Wi-Fi**.
3. Tap the Wi-Fi network you are currently connected to.
4. Scroll down until you see your device's **IP address**.
5. Connect your device to your development machine with a USB cable.
6. Open **Terminal** (command prompt on Windows) and enter the following command:

    `adb tcpip 5555`

7. Disconnect your device from the development machine.
8. Again in **Terminal** (command prompt on Windows), enter the following command replacing the listed IP address with that of your device:

    `adb connect 192.168.254.12:5555`

9. Your device can now be tested across a Wi-Fi network. When you are done testing via Wi-Fi, open **Terminal** (command prompt on Windows) and enter the following command:

   ```
   abd disconnect 192.168.254.12:5555
   ```

Setting up source control

Xamarin Studio comes equipped with integrated source control, including support for both subversion and Git-based repositories. Even if you don't intend to use the integrated source control features of Xamarin Studio, I still recommend that you set it up so your Solution Explorer can reflect the current version control state of the files in your project.

Whether you are using subversion or Git, if you are running on a Windows machine, you will need to install the respective plugin. Also, each option requires access to an outside repository. Refer to your source control provider's documentation for instructions on setting up an account and installing any required plugins.

Once your development machine is ready to support your choice of source control, the process of setting it up in Xamarin Studio differs only slightly between subversion and Git. Since I use Git for all of my projects, I will demonstrate setting up a Git repo within Xamarin Studio by using the following steps:

1. Within Xamarin Studio, go to **Version Control | Checkout**.
2. Select the **Connect to Repository** tab.
3. From the **Type** drop-down list, choose **Git**.
4. In the **Url** field, enter the URL to your repository.
5. If the repository you have chosen is a valid Git repo, all of the remaining fields will populate automatically. Otherwise, complete the remaining fields as required.
6. At the bottom of the form, choose a target directory for your local working copy.

Installing and Setting Up Xamarin Studio

7. When you are done, your dialog box should resemble the following screenshot:

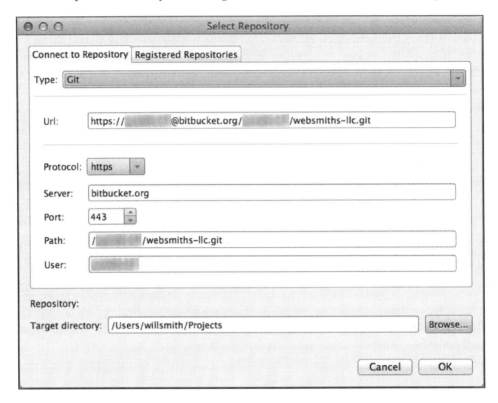

8. Click **OK**.
9. Enter your repo credentials when prompted.
10. After your repository finishes downloading, you can close the dialog box.

> Although I use BitBucket for my projects, there are other excellent Git providers available including GitHub, CodeBase, and many more. Be sure to research what each provider offers in the way of services and cost before making your decision, though. Once you select a source control provider you'll find that your choice becomes embedded in the life of your project, and changing it is not a simple matter.

Additional resources for cross-platform developers

As you work with Xamarin Studio, you will undoubtedly have questions about the software and cross-platform development in general. However, you are equally likely to find unique shortcuts and efficiency hacks that others haven't thought of. Therefore, I strongly recommend that you begin to familiarize yourself with the various documentation repositories, forums, and blogs that relate to the technology you are going to be working with so you can give and take with the community.

Xamarin resources

Xamarin Developer Center is your launching point to documentation, code examples, and training videos provided by the Xamarin team (`http://docs.xamarin.com`).

Xamarin Forums are an excellent place to start. You can sign up using the same login you used to download Xamarin Studio. Take time on a regular basis to read through the posts. You will be amazed by the development gems you will pick up, even from casually reviewing the topics (`http://forums.xamarin.com`).

Xamarin's Bugzilla server is an important site to become familiar with. If you find bugs in the software, this site will help you inform the community. Likewise, you can research a bug to see if someone else has already posted it; if so, see whether a workaround exists until a fix can be pushed out (`https://bugzilla.xamarin.com`).

Third-party resources

In addition to the Apple Developer Program, you should familiarize yourself with the Apple Developer Library, which contains documentation on developing all things on Apple (`https://developer.apple.com/library/`).

The iTunes University offers many resources on iOS and mobile development completely free of charge (`https://www.apple.com/apps/itunes-u/`).

Android Developer Library contains a wealth of information on mobile development. If you are new to Android development, take the time to review the **App Fundamentals** tutorial at `https://developer.android.com/guide/index.html`.

GenyMotion provides some of the fastest Android emulators for app testing and presentation (`http://www.genymotion.com/`).

Summary

In this chapter, we evaluated the prices and options offered by Xamarin Studio and we walked through installing Xamarin Studio and the secondary software needed for cross-platform development. Next, we learned how to enroll in the various developer programs available to cross-platform developers. Finally, we discussed how to set up the basic functions of our development environment, including how to set up simulators and emulators for development testing and integrating source control.

In *Chapter 2, Learning and Customizing the XS Environment*, you will create your first iOS and Android applications. Building and customizing those applications will serve as a context to examine the Xamarin Studio environment in more detail.

Learning and Customizing the XS Environment

In this chapter, we will cover the following topics:

- The Xamarin Studio IDE
- Creating your first iOS application
- Creating your first Android application
- Solution explorer
- Design and information pads
- Menus
- Solution and project options
- Environment preferences

In *Chapter 1*, *Installing and Setting Up Xamarin Studio*, we walked through the somewhat lengthy process of installing Xamarin Studio and the secondary tools that you'll need for effective cross-platform mobile development. Now, we need to familiarize ourselves with the tools that are available in the IDE. Rather than simply walking through the entire interface feature by feature, it's typically easier (and far less boring) to learn the environment in the context of hands-on demonstrations. In addition, there are certain features we simply can't view outside the context of a working solution. Therefore, let's begin by creating a couple of rudimentary applications. Following this, we will fill in the gaps of our knowledge by reviewing the interface features and then editing some project settings. Finally, we'll examine how we can tweak the workspace to maximize your working efficiency.

The Xamarin Studio IDE

Xamarin Studio's **Integrated Development Environment (IDE)** is similar to other IDEs you might have used in terms of functionality and layout. When you open a project, you will see many familiar components. As seen in the following screenshot, the editor window makes up a bulk of the IDE. This is where you will write and edit your code files, set breakpoints for debugging, and stare endlessly for hours asking yourself why you decided to become a software engineer instead of listening to your mother.

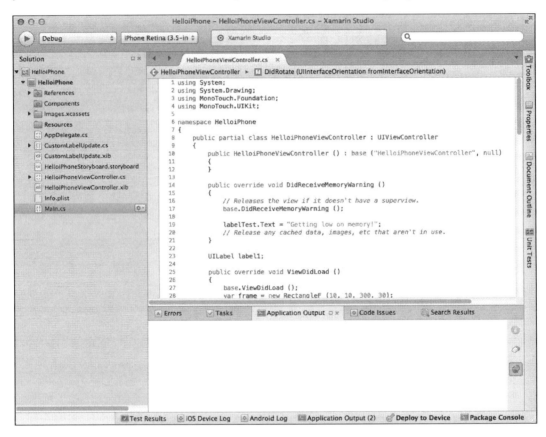

On the left-hand side (by default) the **Solution** pad serves the same purpose as the Solution Explorer in Visual Studio or the Project Navigator in Xcode. This tool displays your files and project architecture, and provides the visual context for the source control object status. At the top of the IDE is the information window. When you build and run your app, this window will display the build's status and any errors or warnings that are encountered.

Various other tool pads and context windows exist or will appear based on the state of your workflow. These will be discussed in detail later in this chapter. For the most part, each of these units of the Xamarin Studio IDE functions exactly as they would in any other IDE. Before we delve into exploring each component in detail, it will help to have a working environment to poke around in, so let's build a pair of quick and dirty applications for this purpose.

Creating your first iOS application

Creating your first iOS application with Xamarin Studio is remarkably easy. For now, let's just build a simple project as a point of reference, as shown in the following steps. We'll dig into the details later.

1. Within Xamarin Studio, navigate to **File** | **New** | **Solution...**.
2. Choose the **C#** | **iOS** | **iPhone** group.
3. Choose the **Single View Application** project type.
4. Name your project `HelloiPhone` and click **OK**.
5. Open the `HelloiPhoneViewController.cs` file.
6. We'll explore some code examples in detail later, but for now just replace the `ViewDidLoad()` method with the following block of code:

    ```
    UILabellabelHello;
    public override void ViewDidLoad ()
            {
    base.ViewDidLoad ();
    var frame = new RectangleF(10, 10, 300, 30);
    labelHello = new UILabel(frame);
    labelHello.Text = "Hello, iPhone!";
    View.Add (labelHello);
            }
    ```

7. In the target dropdown, select **iPhone Retina (4-inch) -> iOS 7.1**.
8. Click the **Build and Run** button.

That's it! You've created your first iOS application using Xamarin Studio! Yes it's merely a simple `Hello World` variation, but this application proves that your environment is properly configured (assuming it ran, of course) and gives us an iOS context to work within.

Learning and Customizing the XS Environment

Creating your first Android application

Surprisingly, creating your first Android application in Xamarin Studio is slightly simpler than creating the iOS counterpart. I wouldn't get too excited, though, because that's normally not the case. Let's create an Android application:

1. Within Xamarin Studio navigate to **File** | **New** | **Solution...**.
2. Choose the **C#** | **Android** group.
3. Keep it simple and choose the **Android Application** project type.
4. Name your project and click **OK**.
5. Click the **Build and Run** button.
6. Choose the emulator you want to target.

> If your emulator hasn't started, the build may succeed but deployment will most likely fail the first time. This is because the Xamarin Studio deployment will timeout if the emulator doesn't return a response quickly enough. The fix is typically very easy, though. Simply wait for the emulator to finish booting up before trying to build and run again.

The Solution pad

Now that we have a project to work with, let's examine the **Solution** pad in detail. The **Solution** pad, as seen in the following screenshot, provides you with an organized view of your project properties and files, as well as an interface to access contextual commands related to them. Projects and files are displayed in a tree view, while a project name displayed in bold represents the startup project.

[42]

You can select individual items or multiple items in a single project or span multiple projects in order to perform batch operations. When you select an individual file, you will notice a small button to the right of the highlighted file. This button opens a context menu where you can open files, add and remove objects, perform management tasks, and work with source control for the highlighted object.

Design pads

Documents and objects selected in the **Solution** pad can be examined in detail using the **Properties** pad. Important details such as **Build action**, **Copy to output directory**, and **Target directory** are all included along with other details, as shown in the following screenshot. This tool serves the same general purpose as the **Properties** window in Visual Studio, although it does not contain all of the same information.

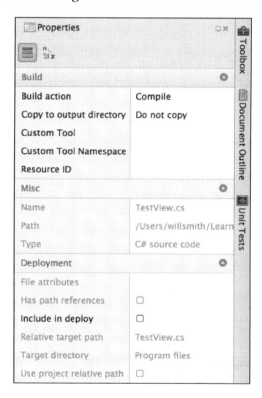

The **Toolbox** pad serves two functions. First, when viewing code files, the toolbox provides a drag-and-drop interface for numerous code snippets. You can also customize the toolbox by adding new snippets from outside assemblies. Secondly, when working in the designer, the toolbox provides instances of layout and control objects that can also be dragged-and-dropped into the visual designer.

The **Document Outline** pad displays the object tree for the document in the editor window. This tree includes all of the classes, properties, methods, and events defined in the open document, and can be used to quickly navigate through large files.

Finally, the **Unit Test** pad is a simple interface that displays each of the unit tests you have defined in your project, while the **Test Results** pad will let you view the output results when those tests are run. You have the option to single out individual tests or run all the tests in the project. Xamarin Studio's unit testing is based on the popular NUnit package, so many of the features found in NUnit can be used in your code testing here.

> For more information on unit testing in Xamarin Studio, please refer to the documentation found at http://docs.xamarin.com/guides/ios/deployment,_testing,_and_metrics/touch.unit/.

Information pads

Xamarin Studio shares many of the same information windows you will find in other IDEs. At any given time in your workflow you will be able to view the **Errors** and **Tasks** pads, as shown in the following screenshot. Any errors, warnings, or messages that the compiler finds in your code will be listed in the **Errors** window. From within the **Errors** pad, you will also be able to access the **Build Output** window, which lists all of the messages generated during a build operation. The **Tasks** pad displays the TODO comments found anywhere in your solution, plus any custom tasks you define. This functionality can be invaluable in ensuring critical features and components are finalized or cleaned up before release, especially in large projects.

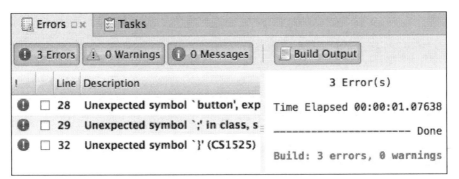

You will also be able to view the **Help**, **Database Browser**, **DeviceLog** (iOS and Android versions), and **Code Issues** pads at any time in your workflow. The **Help**, **Database Browser**, and **Device Log** pads function as their names suggest. **Code Issues** is a tool that will evaluate your code looking for potential warnings and bad practices such as unused objects and redundant declarations or modifiers. Items flagged by the **Code Issues** tool typically have very minimal impact on the final quality of your application, if any impact at all. However, this tool can help you create clean, consistent, and professional code, which all developers should strive for.

While your application is running in the debug mode, you will be able to see several additional pads, as seen in the following screenshot:

Chief among these is the **Application Output** window, which is an immensely powerful debugging tool. This window will display messages generated by the compiler and your application, such as **Warnings** and **Errors**, and it includes any messages you define in your code using methods such as `Console.Writeline`, `Debug.Writeline`, and `Assert.Writeline`. Neither the **Application Output** nor **Build Output** windows will clear until the next build operation, which gives you time to review the messages that are generated and even copy them to the system clipboard as needed.

The **Breakpoints** pad displays information about the breakpoints you have set throughout your application. From this interface, you can add and delete breakpoints, enable or disable them, set conditions, and define special actions to be taken when those conditions are met. Using breakpoints also enables you to take advantage of the remaining pads, because these pads only work when code execution is paused.

The **Locals** pad lets you inspect variables and values within the current execution context and **Watch** lets you add your own variables at runtime and inspect their values. The **Threads** pad allows you to view the status of all the currently running threads in your application.

Call Stack lets you trace your code back from the current point of execution. This can be particularly useful during a crash event, but it can also be very helpful in tracking down bugs that don't result in a crash. Finally, a special pad called the **Immediate** window allows the developer to enter expressions to be evaluated by the development language during debugging. Specifically, it can be used to debug and evaluate expressions, execute statements, print variable values, and so on.

Application, File, and Edit menus

On Mac machines, the first menu you'll see is the **Xamarin Studio** menu, also known as the application menu, as shown in the following screenshot:

Now, let's discuss the various options displayed in the preceding screenshot:

- **About Xamarin Studio** and **Check for updates...**: These options are self-explanatory, although it should be noted that they are found under the **Help** menu on Windows machines.
- **Preferences...**: This opens the **Xamarin Studio Preferences** dialog, which will be discussed in detail later in this chapter. The Windows counterpart to **Preferences...** is **Options...** and is found under the **Tools** menu in Windows environments.

- **Custom Policies...**: This opens the **Custom Policies** dialog, which allows you to set **Source Code** and **Version Control** defaults for your personal environment. **Custom Policies** is also found under the **Tools** menu in Windows environments.

- **Add-in Manager...**: This is very similar to the Visual Studio version. This dialog allows you to install add-ins to Xamarin Studio from a file or from the Internet. Many add-ins require an Indie subscription or higher before they can be installed. **Add-in Manager** is found under the **Tools** menu in Windows environments.

- **Account...**: This item allows you to enter your Xamarin Studio account information. This dialog is strictly for the purpose of licensing and has no bearing on your applications. **Account** is found under the **Tools** menu in Windows environments.

File menus are fairly standardized across applications and platforms, so we won't examine the options found here. This is also mostly true for the **Edit** menu, as shown in the following screenshot:

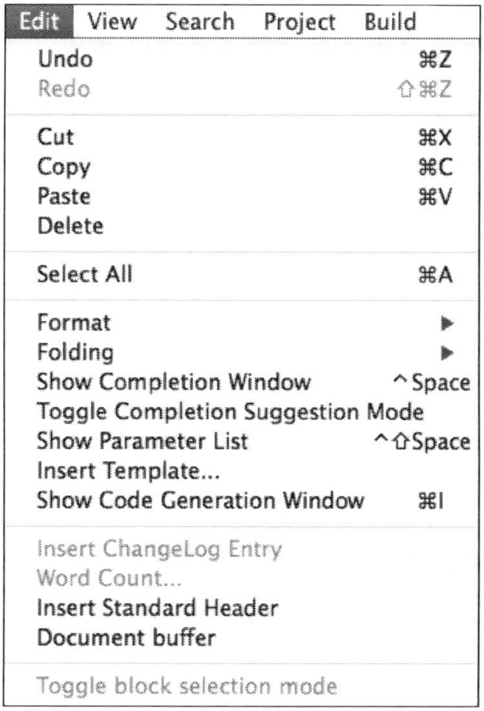

There are at least two items worth our attention in the **Edit** menu:

- **Insert Template...**: This item opens a template dialog. Choosing an item from this dialog will insert a code snippet into your code.
- **Insert Standard Header**: This will prepend a custom header comment to your current code file.

View and Search menus

The following screenshot shows the options of the **View** menu:

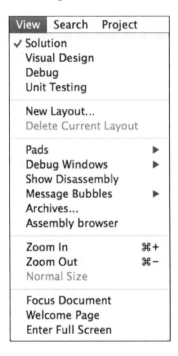

The **View** menu contains many familiar options that are self-explanatory. However, there are three items that are worth reviewing:

- **Show Disassembly**: This opens the **Disassembly** window, which shows the assembly code corresponding to the instructions created by the compiler.
- **Archives...**: This displays a detailed history of release builds created for delivery to the App or Google Play stores.
- **Focus Document**: This moves the current document in the editor pane to bring the cursor into focus.

Next up is the **Search** menu, as shown in the following screenshot:

Likewise, most of the items under the **Search** menu are either familiar or self-explanatory with a few exceptions as follows:

- **Go to File...**: This lets you navigate to any file by selecting it from an alphabetized list of all the files in your solution. When you are working with large or unfamiliar projects with hundreds of files, this is a pretty handy tool to have around.

- **Go to Type...**: This is very similar to **Go to File...** except that it only applies to class definition files in your solution.

- **Inspect**: The **Inspect** submenu group lets you easily navigate through warnings and errors in your code files.

The Project menu

The **Project** menu, shown in the following screenshot, provides access to project level functions and commands:

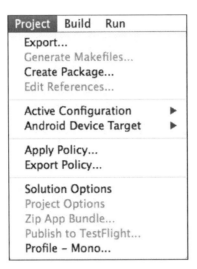

The options in the **Project** menu are as follows:

- **Generate Makefiles...**: This allows you to create makefiles for your solution. See the discussion under the *Project Options* heading later in this chapter for more information about makefiles.
- **Create Package...**: This lets you create an installer package from the files in your solution.
- **Edit References...**: This opens the reference editor dialog, where you can define project references to external packages, .NET assemblies, and other projects within your solution.
- **Active Configuration**: This lets you choose the current build configuration for the selected project.
- **Android Device Target**: This is available for both Android and iOS solutions at the time of writing this, but is only functional for Android solutions. This menu allows you to choose a device emulator before you run the application.
- **Apply Policy...**: This lets you choose editor and version control policies from those bundled with Xamarin Studio, or files you have previously created using **Export Policy...**.
- **Export Policy...**: This lets you save your current project policies to an external file.

- **Solution Options**: This opens the **Solutions Options** dialog window, discussed in depth later in this chapter.
- **Project Options**: This opens the **Project Options** dialog window for the currently selected project. Note that on Mac development machines, this menu item will be labeled **<Project Name> Options**. The **Project Options** dialog window is also discussed in depth later in this chapter.
- **Publish to TestFlight...**: This opens the TestFlight publication dialog. TestFlight will be discussed in depth in *Chapter 8, Deployment*.
- **Zip App Bundle...**: This creates a zipped bundle of your entire solution. This option is only available under iOS solutions.
- **Profile – Mono...**: This opens the integrated Xamarin Memory Profiler tool for iOS solutions. Note that this tool is very similar to Instruments in Xcode, but is only available with a Xamarin Studio Business subscription or higher.

Build and Run menus

Although most developers are familiar with using the few options available in the **Build** menu, it doesn't hurt to briefly review the differences between each of these commands:

The options in the **Build** menu are as follows:

- **Build**: We will perform an incremental build of your solution or project. If the compiler sees no reason for an object or project to be rebuilt, it will be skipped. If you have a large complex project, then the **Build All** command can sometimes be much faster than **Rebuild All**.
- **Rebuild**: This will clean and then build a solution or project completely from scratch, ignoring everything that was built previously.

Learning and Customizing the XS Environment

- **Clean**: This will remove all build artifacts from previous builds in the /bin and /obj directories. Occasions when you've made changes to your code but you're still seeing old behavior is a good example of when you need to clean your project.
- **Stop**: This option will halt a build or rebuild operation.

The **Run** menu shown in the following screenshot contains the developer's most often used commands, certainly for debugging an application:

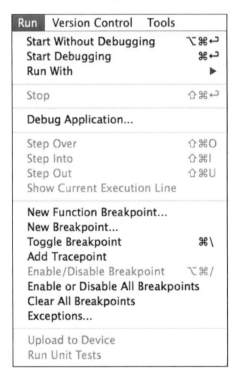

Although many developers will use shortcut keys or toolbar buttons for the following commands, it pays to review their functions in the context of this menu:

- **Start**: This will start the execution of your application with or without debugging, using your target configuration mode and deployment platform.

- **Run With**: This allows you to start and run your application with a specific simulator or emulator. This can also be accomplished by selecting the target from the IDE menu bar and clicking the **Run** button.
- **Stop**: This option will halt the execution of the application in any mode.
- **Debug Application...**: This lets you open an existing application, executable for the purposes of debugging.
- **Step Over**: This instructs the debugger to treat a function as a single unit, executing the entire function and then halting execution at the first line of code outside the function. This means that the application will break on the next statement inside the current function, regardless of whether the current statement is a call to another function. Use **Step Over** if you want to avoid looking inside function calls.
- **Step Into**: This instructs the debugger to execute the next line of code. This option executes the call itself, and then halts execution at the first line of code inside the function. Use **Step Into** when you want to look inside function calls.
- **Step Out**: This will return the execution of your code to the point of the calling function. Use **Step Out** when you are inside a function call and want to return to the calling function.
- **Breakpoint**: The various **Breakpoint** commands allow you to set, disable, delete, and customize breakpoints in your application. However, this interface is slow and awkward compared to using the **Breakpoints** pad discussed earlier in this chapter.
- **Add Tracepoint**: This lets you drop a tracepoint at the current line of code. A tracepoint is simply a breakpoint with a custom action associated with it. Tracepoints work much like the `Trace` function, but without the need to modify your code.
- **Exceptions...**: This opens the **Exception** dialog, which lets you choose specific system exceptions to halt execution on. This feature can be useful when you are researching crashes with little or no evidence of their source.
- **Upload to Device**: This lets you manually deploy your application to an emulator or device.
- **Run Unit Tests**: This executes any unit tests you have defined in your solution.

Learning and Customizing the XS Environment

The Version Control menu

The **Version Control** menu, shown in the following screenshot, provides access to source control integration within Xamarin Studio:

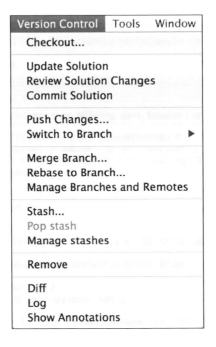

It's important to note that the operation of several of these functions is context-specific, based on the type of source control provider you're using. For example, **Commit Solution** has a very different meaning between a Git repo and a **Subversion** (**SVN**) repo, and if you're working in an environment that utilizes both Git and Subversion, you had better be certain you know the difference!

For an excellent book on Git, try *Git: Version Control for Everyone, Ravishankar Somasundaram, Packt Publishing* (`http://www.packtpub.com/git-version-control-for-everyone/book`).

The **Version Control** menu has the following options:

- **Checkout…**: Depending on your VC provider, this option will either change the current working branch (Git) or download a remote repository (SVN).
- **Update Solution**: This gets and merges the latest code changes from a remote SVN repo to your local working folder.
- **Commit Solution**: This will either create a commit point in your local branch (Git) or upload and merge your changes to the remote repo (SVN).
- **Push Changes…**: This pushes all commits in your local Git repo to the remote.
- **Switch to Branch**: This will change the current working branch.
- **Merge Branch…**: This will merge another branch with your working folder changes. Merge is a universal source control operation, but in my opinion the actual process of merging is more painful in some (SVN) than in others (Git).
- **Rebase to Branch…**: This takes a branch point and moves it to a new starting point. Whether you should *ever* use rebase is a point of some discussion among Git users. However, it is certain that you should *never* use this option lightly or without a thorough understanding of its function and the potential consequences.
- **Stash…**: Use this menu to create Git stashes. A stash in Git could be described as a quasi-commit, typically used when you have to switch branches but the code you're currently working with is in a state that you don't want to commit.
- **Pop stash**: This will apply a stash object to your current working branch and then immediately drop it from your stack.
- **Remove**: This will discard a file from a Git repo and immediately delete it from the filesystem.
- **Diff**: This will compare the current working folder version of a file and the last committed version in the repo. This function works in the same way in both Git and SVN.
- **Log**: This will show you the revision history of the current file. This function works in the same way in both Git and SVN.

Learning and Customizing the XS Environment

Tools, Window, and Help menus

The content of the **Tools** menu, seen in the following screenshot, varies greatly between Mac and Windows machines:

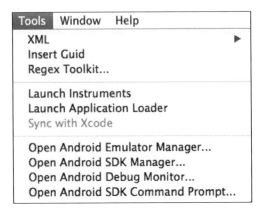

The commands that live in the **Application** menu on a Mac and in the **Tools** menu on Windows machines will not be revisited here:

- **XML**: This submenu group contains commands to work with schemas and XSLT files.
- **Insert Guid**: This will randomly generate and insert a GUID in your code wherever your cursor is located. This tool can be exceptionally useful if you frequently use GUIDs for object identification.
- **Regex Toolkit...**: This will open a regex builder GUI. This bundled tool is similar to many of the regex toolkit extensions you can download for Visual Studio.
- **Launch Instruments**: This will launch the Xcode Instruments utility. This utility will be discussed in more detail in *Chapter 7, Testing and Debugging*.
- **Launch Application Loader**: This is a utility that uploads applications to the Mac/iOS App Store. This utility will be discussed in depth in *Chapter 8, Deployment*.
- **Sync with Xcode**: If for some reason your changes to .xib files in Xcode do not automatically update in Xamarin Studio, or if you have reason to believe they are out of date, **Sync with Xcode** will forcibly update those links.

The items in the **Window** menu are about as universal as you can get, so we'll skip that menu altogether. Contents of the **Help** menu change slightly based on platform, but most of the items are shared between both platforms:

- **API Documentation**: This will link you to the online docs for the Mono Framework.
- **Open Log Directory**: This will take you to the system folder on your local development machine where the Xamarin Studio logs are stored.
- **Report a bug**: This will take you to Xamarin's Bugzilla service where you can enter and research potential defects and other odd behavior you might encounter while working with Xamarin Studio.

Solution Options

To view the **Solution Options** dialog (or **Solution Properties** on Windows machines), shown in the following screenshot, right-click the solution object in the **Solution** pad and choose **Options** from the context menu, or simply double-click the solution object. Alternately, you can go to **Project | Solution Options**. Inside the **Solution Options** dialog there are five groups of settings.

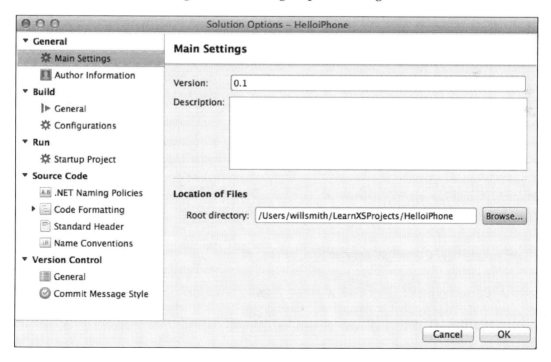

The General group

The **General** group contains the **Main Settings** pane and the **Author Information** pane. **Main Settings** consists of your application's version number, description, and the root directory for the solution on your local machine. **Author Information** allows you to override the default information and enter your own information. Both of these panes are informational and have little impact on the function or deployment of your application.

The Build and Run groups

Under the **Build** group, we find several very important settings. The **General** pane lists the output directory of your application, while the **Configurations** pane allows you to define custom build configuration modes (such as **Debug** and **Release**) and map individual projects to those configurations. The **Run** group contains the **Startup Project** information pane, which allows you to define one or multiple startup projects for your solution.

The Source Code group

The **Source Code** group allows you to set solution-specific properties for your code. The .NET Naming Policies let you customize your namespace organization. In most everyday development scenarios, it's not necessary to define custom source code properties with this level of granularity. However, if you're working on multiple projects and each project has differing coding standards, you'll find that these solution-level options can save you a lot of time and frustration.

Standard Header allows you to define a custom default header comment for each of your new files. This comment recognizes smart tags that can import things such as your name, e-mail address, and company name from the **Main Settings** group, as well as other assembly information. The **Name Conventions** subgroup allows you to define solution-level conventions for your objects. Finally, the **Code Formatting** subgroup allows you to define C#, Text, and XML styles for the entire solution.

The Version Control group

The **Version Control** group will be discussed in greater detail later in this chapter, so for now we'll just examine the options provided in the **Solution Options** dialog. The **General** pane simply exposes the option to disable **Version Control** for the entire solution. The **Commit Message Style** subgroup allows you to create your own default commit message header.

Project Options

The **Project Options** window, as shown in the following screenshot, can be accessed by selecting a project in the **Solution** pad, and then right-clicking it and choosing **Options**, or simply double-clicking the project. Alternately, go to **Project | Project Options**.

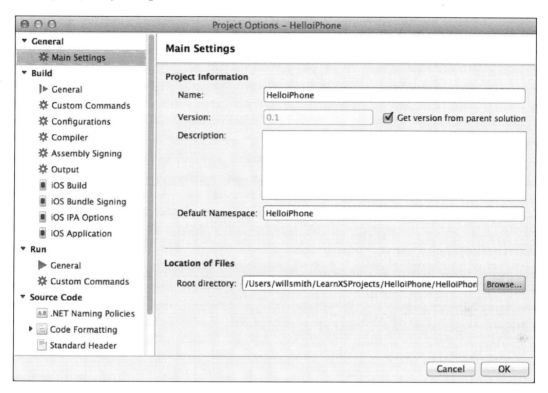

The General group

Under the **General** group, the **Main** pane is very similar to that of its **Solution** options counterpart. The only major difference is that at the **Project** level, you have the option to search for and automatically include new files when the project loads.

Unique to the **Project Options** dialog is the **Makefile integration** pane. Using this pane, you can add settings to synchronize file lists and references to variables in makefiles, plus you can invoke Makefile targets to perform builds.

> **What is a Makefile?**
>
> Right now, depending on your programming background, you could be asking yourself what a makefile is. A makefile is really just a form of a configuration file that contains shell commands and works in conjunction with a Unix utility called **Make**.
>
> Make maintains a list of file dependencies and keeps track of the last time files were updated. Following a build operation, Make recursively compares these two lists to coordinate a cascading build operation throughout the project, updating any files based on the dependencies lists. This process is similar to that of the project build order settings in Visual Studio, only on a much more granular level. Prior to the introduction of makefiles, any change to a project or file required you to recompile any dependent projects and files manually. As you can imagine, if you were working with a large and complex solution, this could quickly become a complex and time-consuming task.
>
> Luckily, Xamarin Studio, much like Visual Studio, takes care of this complexity for us. So if you weren't familiar with makefiles before now, you probably won't need to worry about this pane at all.

The Build group

The **Build** group is significantly different at the project level than the solution level. For example, while the output directory is defined in the **General** options pane at the solution level, it is defined in the **Output** pane at the project level. Also, there are a number of additional settings at the project level that have no contextual meaning at the solution level.

If you are viewing **Project** options in an iOS solution, you will see an option to use the MSBuild engine, but be aware that this option is only viable for certain project types. If you are viewing **Project** options in an Android solution, you will instead see a **Target Framework** dropdown. **Target Framework** allows you to set the Android version you want your application to target, such as KitKat, Jellybean, and others.

Both iOS and Android projects share the **Code Generation** and **Language Options** subgroups. **Code Generation** allows you to define the target type (**Library**, **Executable**, and so on), the **Main Class**, a Win32 icon if desired, and the **Compiler Code Page** (file encoding). You also have the option of whether or not to reference `mscorlib.dll`.

Language Options allows you to choose the C# language version (encoding) and allow unsafe code.

> For more information on the "unsafe" keyword, please refer to the MSDN documentation on the subject at http://msdn.microsoft.com/en-us/library/t2yzs44b.aspx.

Next is the **Custom Commands** pane. If you are familiar with defining pre- and post-build events in Visual Studio, you will find the function of this utility to be very similar. It is my opinion, however, that the Xamarin Studio utility does a better job than the Visual Studio equivalent. Visual Studio lets you define a list of scripts or build events that will run as a sequential batch process, while Xamarin Studio allows you to define strictly independent commands, each with its own set of execution criteria.

The **Compiler** pane gives you control over compile time settings based around build configuration and target platform type. You can set options for whether or not to generate overflow checks, enable optimizations, and generate XML documentation of your classes and methods (very handy for APIs). You can also determine what debug information is generated, determine which symbols are used, and which platform these settings should target. Under the **Warnings** subgroup, you can determine whether specific warnings should be ignored, and whether or not to treat warnings as errors.

In my personal experience, **Treat warnings as errors** helped train me as a developer to address potential problems as they appeared in my code, rather than waiting until they became release bugs that were difficult to track down. Although there will be times when this setting might slow down your development progress, in my opinion it's typically a good practice to turn it on when feasible to do so.

Assembly Signing allows you to attach a **Strong Name** certificate to your project build. **Output** allows you to change your assembly name and define the output directory.

iOS-specific panes

iOS solutions have four platform-specific panes under the **Build** group. If you are already accustomed to development in Xcode, then most of what you see in these four panes will be familiar to you. First, the iOS **Build** pane allows you to set build options that are specific to iOS applications. This pane is very extensive, so we'll examine it in detail.

The General tab

The **General** tab consists of the following options:

- **SDK Version**: This option lets you use different versions of the SDK that are installed on your build machine, which in turn tells Xamarin.iOS the compiler, linkers, and libraries that should be referenced during the build.

- **Linker Behavior**: This can strip out unused objects from your application during compile to help reduce the size of the executable. Linker is a complex subject and you should not implement this build feature without first understanding the implications. For detailed information on Linker, please refer to Xamarin's documentation at http://docs.xamarin.com/guides/ios/advanced_topics/linker/.

- **Optimize PNG image files for iOS**: This feature enable's Apple's modified PNG crush utility, which tries to reduce the size of PNG files using various compression methods. This technique can reduce the size of your compiled application, but the effects on the image are not lossless. So, evaluate the results before releasing your app with this build feature enabled.

- **Enable debugging**: As the name implies, use this option to enable debugging in your compiled application. Be careful that this option is not enabled in the **Release** mode, however, because the debugging information will increase the size of your compiled application significantly as well as slow down its execution.

- **Enable incremental builds**: Incremental builds improves deployment time by telling Xamarin Studio only to rebuild those components that have changed or depend on a component that has changed. Note that if this option is enabled, your project can only be built by Xamarin Studio.

- **Enable profiling**: This option enables the Xamarin Heapshot Memory Profiler, which is a powerful embedded memory analysis tool. For more information on how to configure this tool, please refer to Xamarin's documentation at http://docs.xamarin.com/guides/ios/deployment,_testing,_and_metrics/monotouch_profiler/.

- **Additional mtouch arguments**: The mtouch utility converts your compiled .NET executable into an iOS application bundle. This tool also handles launching your app into the simulator and deployment to physical devices. Using the textbox, you can include additional command-line options for the mtouch utility. For a detailed list of the commands available, refer to Xamarin's documentation at http://iosapi.xamarin.com/?link=man%3amtouch(1).

The Advanced tab

The **Advanced** tab has the following options:

- **Supported architectures**: It is possible for your application to support multiple processor architectures. This option will allow newer devices to use better optimized code, while still supporting older devices. Beware though, as supporting additional architectures in this manner effectively doubles the size of your application.

- **Use LLVM optimizing compiler**: The LLVM compiler can create smaller and faster compiled code, but the build process is significantly slower as a result.

- **Use Thumb-2 instruction set for ARMv7 and ARMv7s**: Thumb-2 compiled code is even smaller than LLVM compiled code alone. In exchange for this increased compression, there is a chance that your released application will run slower.

- **Enable generic value type sharing**: This option enables shared native variants of generic methods for value types, but will increase the size of your compiled application. For more information on generic value type sharing, see Xamarin's release notes on the subject at http://docs.xamarin.com/releases/ios/xamarin.ios_6/xamarin.ios_6.4/.

- **Use SGen generational garbage collector**: SGen or "Simple Generation" garbage collection is the Mono framework garbage collector. This technology is still experimental at the time of writing this, but if you would like to use it to improve performance in your application, you should read the documentation found at http://www.mono-project.com/Generational_GC.

- **Use the reference counting extension**: If you are using SGen in an iOS application, you should be aware that the interaction between garbage collection and automatic reference counting in Objective-C is a very complex subject. This extension helps the garbage collector work more closely with Objective-C by making it aware of the need for reference counting.

- **Internationalization**: To reduce the size of your compiled application, not all encodings are included by default. If you need support for encodings other than the default, you must use this panel to instruct mtouch to include the necessary assemblies.

The **iOS Bundle Signing** pane allows you to assign a provisioning profile to your application, which is essential for publishing to the App Store. Once you have chosen an identity with a valid provisioning profile, you can enter custom entitlements, custom resource rules, and any additional arguments necessary for your build.

> For more information on these options, refer to Apple's **App Distribution Guide** at https://developer.apple.com/library/ios/documentation/IDEs/Conceptual/AppDistributionGuide/ConfiguringYourApp/ConfiguringYourApp.html.

In order to perform ad hoc deployment or enterprise deployment, you will need an IPA file. An IPA file is simply a ZIP file that includes the application, metadata, images, and icons. Creating an IPA file requires an **Ad-Hoc Provisioning Profile**. You create an ad hoc profile in the same way you create a normal provisioning profile, but instead of choosing **App Store** as the distribution method, you choose **Ad-Hoc**.

Once you have your ad hoc profile, the **iOS IPA Options** pane is preconfigured to help you create the IPA file. Selecting the **Build ad-hoc/enterprise package (IPA)** checkbox is all that is required on this pane, and the remaining fields are optional. To deploy this file to your devices, you only need to build using the ad hoc configuration, and then double-click on the IPA file that is created in the project's /bin/iPhone/Ad-Hoc directory. This will open the file in iTunes, which will let you sync to your device.

Finally, the **iOS Application** pane gives you direct access to the core iOS project settings. These are identical to those found in Xcode projects. You can also access these settings by opening the solution's Info.plist file. In *Chapter 3, Working with Xcode and the Android SDK*, we will take a closer look at these settings from within Xcode. For more information, please refer to the Xcode documentation on project settings at https://developer.apple.com/library/ios/recipes/xcode_help-project_editor/_index.html.

Android-specific panes

Android solutions have two platform-specific panes under the **Build** group. First, the **Android Build** pane allows you to set build options that are specific to Android applications.

The Packaging tab

The **Packaging** tab has the following options:

- **Use shared Mono runtime**: This option creates packages with a dependency on the shared Mono runtime, which allows the package to be built and deployed much faster.

- **Fast assembly deployment**: This option causes the compiler to create packages without assemblies, opting instead to deploy the assemblies directly to the device with your application. The benefit here is that it will improve code redeployment speed after the initial build.

> Although **Fast assembly deployment** is effective in the emulator, it can sometimes fail when deploying to a device, giving the error message **Deployment failed. FastDev directory creation failed.** If you receive this message, disable **Fast assembly deployment** and try to deploy to the device again.

- **Embed assemblies in native code**: As the name suggests, this option will embed your assemblies directly within the native code of your compiled application. Note that this option requires Xamarin.Android Enterprise edition.
- **Uncompressed resource extensions**: By adding a comma-separated list of file extensions to this field, you have the option to leave certain file formats in an uncompressed state. You may want to do this for image files to prevent loss of quality, or other file types that have difficulty being uncompressed on a physical device.

The Linker tab

The **Linker** tab has the following options:

- **Linker behavior**: Linker behavior for Android projects functions in exactly the same way as for iOS projects.
- **Ignore assemblies**: Remember that the Linker tool removes features from managed class libraries that the application is not using in an attempt to reduce the overall application size. There may be times, however, when you don't want to modify specific external assemblies. In that case, you can tell Linker to ignore these assemblies by adding them to this field as a comma-separated list.
- **Internationalization**: Internationalization settings functions the same for Android projects as for iOS projects.

The Advanced tab

The **Advanced** tab has the following options:

- **Supported ABIs**: Android allows machine code that will support multiple CPU architectures. This is achieved by associating the machine code with an **Application Binary Interface (ABI)**. The ABI lists the machine code that can run on a given architecture. This feature is similar to the **Supported architectures** option in an iOS project, except that additional architecture support does not effectively double the size of your compiled application. At the time of writing this, armeabi has the broadest device support, but armeabi-v7a is the newest architecture.

- **Java heap size**: Some of the tools used during the build process require the **Java runtime (JRT)**. The runtime uses a fixed amount of memory during the build process, and sometimes this is insufficient for larger applications. If you find that you are receiving JRT errors during builds, try increasing the heap size using this option.

- **Java arguments**: Any JRT arguments you would normally use when invoking the JRT from the command line can also be introduced into your application build process by entering them in this field.

- **Mandroid arguments**: Mandroid is the utility that builds a package from compiled DLL files and the Android resources in your project. If you need to pass any additional arguments to the utility, enter them here.

Next, you will see the **Android Application** pane, which allows you to modify your package manifest file. You can also access these settings by opening the **AndroidManifest.xml** file from your project's `Properties` folder. In the manifest, you can define both the application name as well as the package name. The application name is the name that will appear in the Google Play Store. You can also choose the application icon, and it is strongly recommended that you do so because some application stores will not let you publish your app without one.

> Note that the Xamarin Studio plugin for Visual Studio 2010 does not permit you to change this setting. To change this value in a Visual Studio environment, you must edit the Icon property of the `ApplicationAttribute` in the `Properties/AssemblyInfo.cs` file, as shown in the following code:
>
> ```
> [assembly: Application(Icon = "@drawable/launch_icon")]
> ```

Version number and version name are your application's primary identifiers, and version name is the value that will appear in the Google Play Store. The details and implementation of your versioning system are completely up to you, but don't spend too much time trying to devise the perfect versioning system because it doesn't exist. Just design a system that works for your application and workflow, stick to it, and be sure to update this field before you release new versions of your app.

Typically, an Android application can only run on a device running the target API or higher. Changing the **Minimum Android version** field allows your application to also run on older devices. You should only change this value when you are very familiar with the framework requirements of your application, and you have explicitly declared runtime checks to ensure your app only uses newer APIs on devices that are new enough to support them. You can also change **Target Android version** to something other than your target framework if your application uses libraries that have a specific target API version.

If you want to allow your application to be installed on external storage, **Install location** allows you to declare your preference in this matter. **Auto** indicates that your application is permitted to be stored on an external storage, but you really don't have a preference either way. This allows the system to decide where to install your app, and the user can also move the app between internal and external storage. If you declare `preferExternal`, you are requesting that your application be installed on an external storage, but there is no guarantee that will happen. Lastly, if you declare **internal**, then your application will definitely be installed on the internal storage.

Finally, the **Required** permissions group allows you to explicitly declare the permissions your application needs to run. These permission settings will be added to the application's manifest file. While installing your app, your end user will be required to grant your application permission to use the various features you selected.

The Run group

Under the **Run** project option group, you can define runtime parameters based on the build configuration and target platform, plus any custom commands. The **General** pane allows you to define parameters, decide whether or not your app should run on an external console, and introduce any environment variables your application requires. The **Custom Commands** panel is similar to that found under the **Build** project options group, except that these commands target the application runtime.

Source Code and Version Control groups

Source code and Version control options at the **Project** level are identical to those at the **Solution** level. On each of these panes, you will see an option called **Policy** or **Version Control Policy**. Typically, these options will be set to **Parent Policy** or **Inherited Policy**, meaning they are inherited from the **Solution** level. If you want to implement specific settings for any particular project, you can change these options to **Custom**.

The iOS projects have one additional pane at the **Project** level under the **Source Code | Code Formatting** subgroup called **Interface Builder file**. This pane allows you to define formatting rules for the XIB and XML files produced by Xcode's interface builder.

Environment preferences

By this point, you may have already found some aspects of the Xamarin Studio UI that don't fit well with your personal workflow. For example, if you're moving from a Windows development environment into a Mac for the first time (as I did when I began using Xamarin Studio), you may find shortcut key mappings on the Mac to be nothing short of irritating. No worries because these mappings, and many other global features within the IDE, can be customized to your taste using the **Preferences** dialog, shown in the following screenshot. To begin working on these settings, we need to open the IDE's **Preferences** dialog. On a Mac, go to **Xamarin Studio | Preferences...**. On a PC, navigate to **Tools | Options...**.

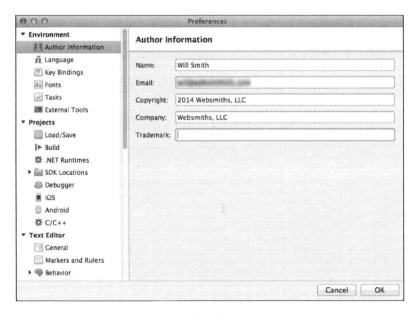

Environment

Under the **Environment** project group, the **Author Information**, **Language**, **Key Bindings**, and **Fonts** panes are self-explanatory. The **Tasks** pane lets you define custom keywords for various tasks, such as TODO and HACK, throughout your solution. Any code comments that begin with a keyword in this pane will be gathered together in the **Tasks List** window underneath the editor. Finally, the **External Tools** pane can be used to add custom functionality to your IDE through third-party command-line utilities.

Projects

The **Projects** group contains a number of options that you might never use, or you might set once and never again, so it's a good idea to set these options early on. **Load/Save** lets you choose your default project file format and solution location. The **.NET Runtimes**, **Apple**, and **Android SDK Locations** panes list file paths for the utilities of the same name. The **Debugger** pane lets you define rules for how the bundled debugger functions. The **iOS** pane gives you the additional option to debug iOS apps over Wi-Fi, and the Android pane lets you define additional command-line arguments to launch the emulator. Finally, the C/C++ pane lets you choose the default C and C++ compilers that will be used during builds.

Text Editor

When we speak of customizing the development environment, in most cases we're probably thinking about the options found under the **Text Editor** group. Within the **General** pane, in addition to being able to define code-folding behavior and whether or not to use antialiasing in your font, you can set a value for **Line ending conversion**. This option may seem insignificant at first glance, but text file line endings are one of those obscure fundamental differences between Unix and Windows. As such, if you find yourself working on linked code files between a Mac and a PC, you will want to address this option at some point.

In the **Behavior** pane, you can set automatic behaviors for code completion, define your default indentation mode, and define word break modes. The **Behavior** pane also has a subpane for XML code. **Syntax Highlighting** is where you can choose or modify the editor window's color scheme. The **Code Templates** pane allows you to modify and create code snippets that appear in the **Toolbox** pad.

Learning and Customizing the XS Environment

The **Source Analysis** pane lets you enable source analysis of files opened in the editor. If you are not familiar with static source analysis, it's similar to having another developer looking over your shoulder and reviewing code as you write it, looking for warnings and errors before they become actual problems. If Xamarin Studio finds a potential issue in your code, it is flagged in the editor and a marker is added to the scroll bar.

Lastly, in the **Text Editor** group, the **XML Schemas** pane lets you add new XML schema files and map your file extensions. This mapping is critical to the IDE's ability to properly parse your code on the fly.

Source Code, Version Control, Other, and Packages groups

Most of what is found under the **Source Code** group is identical to the **Solution** and **Project** level options, except that the settings found here are the global defaults. However, under the **C#** subgroup, there are two additional panes. First, the **Code Inspection** pane that lets you define global filters for common practices and code improvement, and how the **Code Inspection** window will color code instances of these rules. Secondly, the **Context Actions** pane allows you to select rules for code completion and autocorrect.

The **Version Control** group is also similar to its **Solution** and **Project** level counterparts, with the additional option to disable version control globally in the IDE under the **General** pane. Finally, under the **Other** group, the **Log Agent** pane allows you to choose whether or not to automatically submit error diagnostic and usage information to Xamarin. Since F# support was added in Xamarin 3, Xamarin Studio 5 added the **F# Settings** pane to the **Other** group. In the **F# Settings** pane, you can choose the **F# Interactive framework**, **compiler type**, and several basic font options.

Newly added to the **Preferences** dialog in Xamarin Studio 5 is the **Packages** group. In the **General** pane, you can set the option to automatically restore packages when opening a solution. Under the **Sources** pane, you can manage external packages such as the NuGet Gallery.

Summary

In this chapter, you were introduced to the Xamarin Studio IDE and you created your first application. We examined the many options to customize the editor, as well as solutions and projects. We also examined the most important menu options within the application.

In the next chapter, we will learn about Xcode and the Android SDK, focusing on the functions that are critical for Xamarin Studio developers to understand.

3
Working with Xcode and the Android SDK

In this chapter, we will cover the following topics:

- Introduction to Xcode
- Outlets and Actions
- Creating a ViewController in Xcode
- XIB, NIB, DESIGNER, and STORYBOARD files
- Android SDK Manager
- Xamarin Studio Designer for iOS
- Creating a storyboard in Xamarin Studio
- Xamarin Studio Designer for Android
- Creating a Layout in Xamarin Studio

Now that you have Xamarin Studio set up and working, we'll take a little time to examine the third-party tools you will be using on a regular basis. First, we'll look at iOS development using Xcode with Xamarin Studio, paying particular attention to the Xcode IDE and Objective-C components we need to understand in order to bind our view controllers to our .NET code files. Next, we'll examine the Android SDK and learn about layout design and implementation. Following this, we'll look at the iOS and Android designers that come bundled with Xamarin Studio 5. Finally, you'll create some quick applications to apply what you've learned.

Introduction to Xcode

Although Xamarin Studio 5 introduced a graphical designer of its own for iOS and Mac development, the IDE is still capable of utilizing Xcode's **Interface Builder** for the development of view controllers and other user interface components. Through the course of this chapter, we'll look at using both tools. We'll begin with Xcode's Interface Builder because I feel that understanding how Xcode functions will help you better understand the design and functionality of the Xamarin Studio designer. The following screenshot provides a basic breakdown of Xcode's layout:

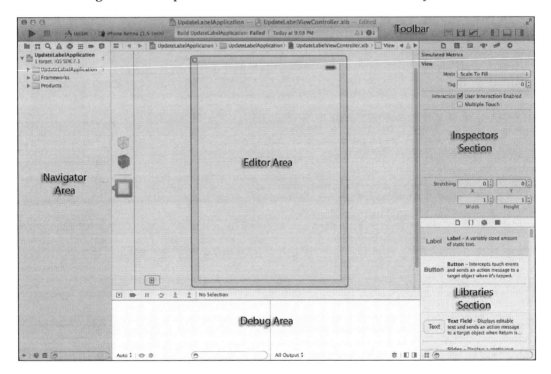

 If you find a control or interface that you need to know more about, you can easily find the help article for it by holding *Ctrl* and clicking on the interface.

Toolbar

The toolbar area runs along the top of the IDE, and it contains some of the most commonly used controls. On the left-hand side of the toolbar are the controls to run or halt the execution of the application. Clicking the play button will start or restart the application if it is already running. Next, there is a breadcrumb control that lets you select a target simulator or device for the application to be executed on. If you happen to be working in a workspace, this breadcrumb control will also let you choose a project to start. A workspace is a collection of projects, similar to a solution in .NET terms. Since development in Xamarin only uses Xcode as a platform to visually design view controllers, it's unlikely you will work with multiple projects within Xcode.

At the center of the toolbar is the message window. This displays messages about anything Xcode is doing while we work with our project. Typically, these messages will include build status and quick links to warnings or errors found by the compiler.

To the right-hand side of the message window there are two groups of three buttons. The first group determines the editor view we are currently using. The first of these buttons enables the standard editor, which allows you to work on one file in the full editor area. Next, the assistant editor, also known as assistant mode, displays two files of the developer's choice side by side. This mode is particularly useful when working with Objective-C because you can view your header and implementation files side by side. Also, it's almost a requirement in order to work with Interface Builder because it allows you to create Outlets and Actions easily using your mouse. Lastly, if your project is under source control, the version editor allows you to review code changes since your last commit operation.

The second group of three buttons allows you to show or hide the navigator, debug, and utility areas, respectively.

The navigator area

Before examining the navigator area, be aware that the hierarchy of projects and objects in an Xcode workspace is somewhat different than that of Visual Studio or Xamarin Studio. For the purpose of our discussions, there are two main differences you should be aware of. First, the concept of a solution, which is a collection of projects in Visual Studio and Xamarin Studio, is represented by a workspace in Xcode. Project objects are basically the same in both environments.

Secondly, be aware that an object's position in the project tree does not necessarily represent its location in the filesystem. Folders in the Xcode project tree are referred to as groups, and they might or might not map to a matching folder in the filesystem. This is especially important to understand when you are adding new files to your project through Xcode, because your assumptions on where the files will be created in the filesystem could be wrong. When in doubt, right-click on an object and choose **Show in Finder** to be sure. You can avoid this complication altogether by simply adding all of your new files and resources from within Xamarin Studio.

The navigator area is your tool to navigate everything in and about your project or workspace. There are eight different navigators available, and they can each be selected by choosing one of the buttons aligned across the top of the area. Each navigator also provides a series of context-specific functions along the bottom of the area. Not all of these navigators, shown in the following screenshot, are relevant to our discussions concerning Xamarin Studio:

These navigators are defined as follows:

- **Project navigator**: This is normally visible when you open Xcode. From this navigator, you can access all the groups, files, resources, and configuration settings for the entire project or workspace. Simply clicking a file from the project navigator will open that file in the editor area. Code files (those that end with .h or .m) will open in the text editor, interface design files (with file extension .xib) will open in Interface Builder, and a project header will open the project editor. The context-specific functions in this area include tools to add new files, display only the most recently modified files, list objects by source control status, and filter objects by name. Realistically, this is the only Xcode navigator you will absolutely need to use as a Xamarin.iOS developer.

- **Symbol navigator**: This is a fairly common utility in any IDE, and allows you to browse the symbols available in your project.

- **Find navigator**: This allows you to search for strings in your Xcode project. This is similar in function to using **Search all files and folders** in Visual Studio.

- **Issue navigator**: This displays all of the warnings and errors found in your code. Since you won't be compiling and running your apps from Xcode, you won't use this navigator very often, if at all.

- **Test navigator**: This displays a list of unit tests defined in your project. It provides a simple interface to run single tests or groups of tests, and also displays the results of those tests. Since the majority of our code will be written in .NET, unit tests will normally be defined in Xamarin Studio using the Unit.Touch framework. For more information on creating unit tests in Xamarin Studio, please refer to *Chapter 7, Testing and Debugging*.
- **Debug navigator**: When an application is running, the debug navigator displays the call stack.
- **Breakpoint navigator**: This displays information on breakpoints and allows you to manually assign new breakpoints to your project.
- **Log navigator**: This displays all of the logged messages produced by the build system and any NSLog (loosely equivalent to Console.Write in .NET) messages defined in your Objective-C code. You may occasionally find a use for this navigator, but typically your most important messages will be logged in Xamarin Studio.

The utility area

To the right-hand side of the editor area is the utility area. The top half of the utility area contains the inspectors section. Inspectors are content sensitive, so you won't always have access to every inspector option. If you are editing a text file, you will only see the File and Quick Help inspectors, but when working with Interface Builder, you will see six inspectors. In our work designing view controllers using Xcode, we will use each of the inspectors in the following screenshot on a regular basis:

These inspectors are defined as follows

- **File inspector**: This provides basic filesystem information. Filename, type, relative location in the filesystem, and full path are all provided here. If you are working with an Interface Builder document, you will see additional options for which a program opens the file, what the file is built for, and how the file is to be viewed. Finally, you will see an option for **Use Auto Layout**. Unchecking the **Use Auto Layout** option will enable the auto-resizing mask, also called the springs and struts model on the Size inspector.

> Using Auto Layout isn't always the way to go, especially if you are trying to design your own custom controls or table view cells. For more information on the Auto Layout keyword, please refer to Apple's iOS Developer Library documentation on the subject at `https://developer.apple.com/library/ios/documentation/userexperience/conceptual/AutolayoutPG/Introduction/Introduction.html`.

- **Quick help inspector**: This displays the reference documentation for any object selected in the file navigator or in the editor area. Quick help is available for symbols in the source editor, for interface objects in Interface Builder, and for build settings in the project editor. This same information is also available in a **Quick Help** window, which can be accessed by holding down the option (*Alt*) key and clicking on an object.

- **Identity inspector**: This allows you to view and manage metadata for an object, such as its accessibility information, runtime attributes, label, and so on. Most importantly for us, the identity inspector allows you to define a **Custom Class** for your view. To access the **Custom Class** field in the Identity inspector, select the File Owner icon on the left edge of the editor area.

- **Attributes inspector**: This provides tools to configure attributes of the selected interface object. The available options are context-specific to the object selected.

- **Size inspector**: This allows you to define characteristics such as the initial size and position, minimum and maximum size, and any auto-sizing rules for the selected object.

- **Connections inspector**: This allows you to view any Outlets and Actions defined for the selected object. This interface also allows you to create new connections or break existing ones.

> You can also access the connections in a context menu by right-clicking the view icon on the left edge of the editor area.

The bottom half of the utility area contains the libraries section. Unlike the inspectors, the library is not context-sensitive and its functions remain consistent no matter what type of file you are working on. There are four libraries, as seen in the following screenshot:

These libraries include the File Template library, Code Snippet library, Object library, and the Media library. For the majority of our work in Xcode, we will use the Object library as this contains the UI elements that we will be dropping into our views during design.

The debug area

At the bottom of the IDE is the debug area. This tool lets you control the execution of your code, view program variables and registers, view its console output, and interact with the debugger. As your applications will typically launch from Xamarin Studio, you may not use this area very often.

The editor area

The editor area is where most development work is performed in Xcode, and it is always visible in the workspace window. This area is marked by several important features for Xamarin developers. First, note the jump bar at the top of the area. This tool provides a sort of breadcrumb interface to select everything from project-level objects down to class-level properties and methods. The configuration and behavior of each jump bar is customized for the context it appears in, so this tool will change based on which editor you are using.

Technically, the editor area comprises nine different editor tools. For the purposes of our work, we are only interested in four of these:

- **Interface Builder**: This is where you will graphically create and edit user interface files.

- **Source editor**: This is where you will write and edit source code for your interface files.

- **Property list**: This editor allows you to view and edit various types of property lists, or plists. Xamarin Studio has its own plist editor so using this tool is optional.

- **Project editor**: This editor lets you view and edit project and target settings, such as build options, target architectures, and code-signing characteristics. As discussed in *Chapter 2, Learning and Customizing the XS Environment*, Xamarin Studio provides its own tool to edit the project settings, so using the Xcode version is optional.

> **How can I customize this workflow?**
>
> By this point you might have noticed that unlike some other development applications, Xcode isn't very configurable in the area of workflow. You cannot rearrange, drag-and-drop, or detach panes from one area to another. That's because this is an Apple program and what you see is what you get. Navigator stays on the left, utility stays on the right, and so on.
>
>
>
> There is, however, some relief in the form of a Safari-style tabbed interface, which allows you to have multiple files open simultaneously in the same workspace. You can open new tabs manually by navigating to **File** | **New Tab**, pressing *Command + T*, or by clicking the add (+) button at the right end of the tab bar. Alternatively, you can set Xcode to automatically open new files in a tab by setting **General Preferences**:
>
> - Open **Xcode** | **Preferences**....
> - Select the **Navigation** panel.
> - Set the **Double Click Navigation** option to **Uses Separate Tab**.
>
> Once you have implemented these steps, you can double-click on the files and have them open in a new tab for easy navigation. If you are coming from a Windows environment, this might not completely resolve your workflow learning curve, but luckily you won't be spending the bulk of your time developing in Xcode.

Outlets and Actions

Outlets and Actions are key concepts to understand when working with Xcode and Xamarin.iOS. Defined in the class header file, these properties allow the `ViewController` to tie into, or interact, with the objects defined in the view. In my opinion, Outlets and Actions are most easily understood in terms of flow of communication. Simply stated, an Outlet allows your `ViewController` to talk to your view, while an Action allows your view to pass messages back to your `ViewController`.

Although the new graphical designer for iOS removes much of the headache from working with Outlets and Actions, it is still a good idea to learn how to create and manage them using Xcode to better understand how they work.

Outlets

An Outlet exposes an object in the view to the corresponding `ViewController`. This allows the `ViewController` to update property values on that object by referencing the Outlet's name. For example, the following bit of code exposes a `UILabel` object:

```
//MYViewController.h file implementation
@interface MYViewController : UIViewController
@property (weak, nonatomic) IBOutlet UILabel *placeholderLabel;
@end

//MyViewControllerCS file (File's Owner)
public override void ViewDidLoad()
{
  placeholderLabel.Text = "I am a placeholder label.";
}
```

> **Downloading the example code**
> You can download the example code files for all Packt books you have purchased from your account at http://www.packtpub.com. If you purchased this book elsewhere, you can visit http://www.packtpub.com/support and register to have the files e-mailed directly to you.

An Outlet is defined as a property with the type qualifier of **IBOutlet**. This can be done manually, but it is easier and smarter to let Xcode create the property and wire up the object for us. We'll examine how in a moment, but at this point just note that you can change the property values on an object defined in your view. Be aware that you can add an Outlet to any object defined in your view.

Actions

Unlike Outlets, Actions are methods, not properties. An Action functions as a messenger from the view to your `ViewController`. Technically speaking, the `ViewController` is set up as **Target** for any Actions defined in the View. An Action's behavior can be thought of in terms of the command pattern found in WPF applications, where user interactions defined in the XAML file are handled in the CS code behind file.

Whenever some kind of event occurs with an object on the view, any actions associated with the event for that object will pass a message on to the `ViewController`. Just as you can share event handlers in C#, you can wire up multiple controls to the same Action in iOS. Strictly speaking, the words "event" and "handler" are not correct in this context, but since we are predominantly working in .NET, it's just clearer to think in these terms.

The following bit of code expands our previous code example to add an Action:

```
//MYViewController.h file implementation
@interface MYViewController : UIViewController
@property (weak, nonatomic) IBOutlet UILabel* placeholderLabel;
-(IBAction)updateLabelButtonTouchUpInside:(id)sender;
@end

//MyViewControllerCS file (File's Owner)
public override void ViewDidLoad()
{
  placeholderLabel.Text = "I am a placeholder label.";
}
partial void updateLabelButtonTouchUpInside(NSObject sender)
{
  placeholderLabel.Text = "I have been updated!";
}
```

Now the `TouchUpInside` event is wired to a button defined in our view, and its handler is defined in the file owner.

Adding Outlets and Actions

Adding an Outlet or an Action through Interface Builder is quite simple. Although there are several methods to do this, the easiest way is to use the assistant editor and your mouse.

Open a XIB file in Interface Builder and switch to the assistant editor to open the header file. Next, right-click or command-click on an object in Interface Builder, and while still holding the right mouse button or command key down, drag the mouse over to the `@interface` section of the header file. When you drop the wire in the `@interface` section, you will be prompted to create either an Outlet or an Action. We'll examine this process in detail during the next walkthrough.

Adding a ViewController to our project

Let's manually create a `ViewController` that consists of a label, text field, and button:

1. In Xamarin Studio, create a new solution by going to **iOS** | **Empty Application**, and name it `UpdateLabelApplication`.
2. Right-click on the `UpdateLabelApplication` project and select **Add File...**.
3. Select a file by going to **iOS** | **iPhone View Controller**.
4. Name the file `UpdateLabelViewController` and click on the **New** button.
5. If Xcode does not open Interface Builder automatically, open the file from the Solution Explorer pad.
6. Switch to the assistant view, and open the `UpdateLabelViewController.h` file in the right pane using the jump bar.
7. Using the Object Library in the Utility Area, drag-and-drop a Text Field, Button, and Label control onto the view in the left pane of Interface Builder. Your view should look something like the following screenshot:

8. Holding down the *Ctrl* key, select the text field and drag a wire across to the .h file, releasing just below the `@interface` label.
9. Create an Outlet named `textField`.
10. Drag another wire for the Label control and create an Outlet named `label`.
11. Finally, drag another wire for the Button control and create an Action for the **Touch Up Inside** event named `updateButtonTouchUpInside`.
12. Save your file and switch back to Xamarin Studio.
13. Open the `UpdateLabelViewController.cs` file.
14. Below the `ViewDidLoad` method, type the keyword `partial` and hit the Space bar. Xamarin Studio will provide you with an autocomplete option to create an event handler. Select this option.
15. Inside the new method, replace the default exception code with the following:
    ```
    label.Text = textField.Text;
    textField.Text = "";
    ```
16. Open the `AppDelegate.cs` file from the Solution Explorer pad.
17. Within the `FinishedLaunching` method, replace the existing code with the following code:
    ```
    this.window = new UIWindow (UIScreen.MainScreen.Bounds);

    var viewController = new UpdateLabelViewController();

    this.window.RootViewController = viewController;
    this.window.MakeKeyAndVisible ();
    return true;
    ```
18. Run the application.
19. Type some text into the text field and click the button. The label should get updated with the text you entered, and the text field should be cleared.

How it works

You have created a new `ViewController` using Xamarin Studio and the Xcode Interface Builder. Your view consists of the XIB file, while your `ViewController` consists of three parts, including the header (.h) file, your code behind (CS) file, and a designer (DESIGNER) file generated by Xamarin Studio.

Note that the code behind file is also set as the file owner for the XIB file in Xcode. This is extremely important! This linkage helps Xcode create the appropriate bindings between the view and `ViewController`. The changes you make in the header file in Xcode will automatically sync to Xamarin Studio through the DESIGNER file when you save your work, partly because this linkage exists.

Next, you implemented the `updateButtonTouchUpInside` Action in your code behind file. In this case, you used the Action to manipulate the properties of objects in the view through the Outlets you defined for them.

Finally, you wired up your new view to your application architecture. Since your application was empty when you began, you set this new view as the `rootViewController` to be launched from the `AppDelegate` class. First, your code defines a window for the application, and then you create an instance of your new `ViewController` class. This instance is then set as the window's `RootViewController`, and finally you set the window as visible.

XIB, NIB, DESIGNER, and STORYBOARD files

In the earlier versions of Xcode, the Interface Builder generated NIB files (pronounced Nib). These were not individual files, but were actually directory packages. Most developers who worked with these files would probably agree that directory packages are somewhat complicated to work with, especially with regard to version control. With Xcode 3.1, Apple introduced XIB files (oddly enough, also pronounced Nib). XIB files are flat XML files depicting the layout information of the view. Since they are written in XML, they are much easier to tweak (when necessary), easier to track with source control, and they make reviewing changes between versions simpler. Ultimately, the XIB files are compiled into the `.nib` files prior to deployment, but you won't be able to edit those because they open in Interface Builder as unreadable binary code.

With the introduction of .NET into the mix, Xamarin added DESIGNER files. For lack of a better description, designer files expose your Objective-C header (`.h` file) contents to your .NET code. Outlets and Actions defined in Interface Builder appear in the DESIGNER file in the following format (from the previous `UpdateLabelApplication` example):

```
[Outlet]MonoTouch.UIKit.UILabel label { get; set; }
[Outlet]MonoTouch.UIKit.UITextField textField { get; set; }
[Action ("updateButtonTouchUpInside:")]partial void
  updateButtonTouchUpInside (MonoTouch.Foundation.NSObject
    sender);
```

As you can see from the preceding code, the Outlets are generated as private properties, so they are only accessible to the XIB's file owner. The return types of these properties are the respective MonoTouch.UiKit framework types for each of the objects that the Outlets are wired to in the XIB file. Actions are generated as partial methods (that must be implemented in your CS code behind file). These partial methods are decorated with the `Action` keyword and the name of the Action as defined in the `.h` file. Don't get too concerned about the trailing colon on that name. This is a method naming convention of Objective-C, and it's completely appropriate in this context. Additionally, you will see a method named `ReleaseDesignerOutlets()` that helps out with memory management of the Outlet properties.

There are a couple of other items you should be aware of, concerning XIB and DESIGNER files. First, never edit these files directly. I suppose technically it's possible to muck about in these without throwing a wrench into the works, but it's rarely worth the frustration. In my experience, problems in these files can introduce crashes that produce cryptic Objective-C exception messages coupled with little or no stack trace information. If you want to change something in the XIB or DESIGNER file, open it through Xamarin Studio so you can make your changes in Xcode. Then the DESIGNER file will correctly reflect the current state of the XIB file. While we're on this subject, never open XIB files directly from Xcode, but always through Xamarin Studio. When you open the XIB files from Xamarin Studio, your solution will automatically sync with the new changes when you save your work in Xcode.

Lastly, concerning DESIGNER files, it might be tempting to directly call `ReleaseDesignerOutlets()` when you are dismissing a `ViewController`. Again, it is technically possible to call this method, but you shouldn't do it. Remember that MonoTouch is garbage collected, while modern iOS uses **ARC (automatic reference counting)** and the relationship between the two is very complex. If you want to recycle the memory, just call `Dispose()` and let MonoTouch handle the dirty details.

Newly introduced in Xamarin Studio 5 is the STORYBOARD file and support for designing storyboards graphically. A storyboard is one single file that contains all of the views in your app, allowing you to see the whole story at once. Each `ViewController` and view pair is referred to as a scene. In iPhone terms, it is safe to assume that each scene represents one screen of content. On an iPad, however, multiple scenes can be visible simultaneously using a **Popover View Controller**. The STORYBOARD file also includes the flow of your application, allowing you to add transitions (Apple calls these "segues") between the scenes.

Storyboards are meant to completely replace individual XIB files in your projects, although it's possible to launch a XIB manually from within a storyboard. This would be useful if you are retrofitting or adding storyboards to an existing XIB-based application, or if you simply plan to mix and match XIB files and storyboards in the same app.

The primary advantage to using storyboards is that they will reduce the number of files in your application and minimize the amount of boilerplate code needed to manage multiple views. We'll look at adding storyboards to your application in the next walkthrough.

Xamarin Studio Designer for iOS

Xamarin Studio's Designer for iOS will allow you to create storyboards graphically, and do so more easily than using Xcode because it's streamlined for this specific purpose. Although you cannot create individual XIB files using the Xamarin Studio designer, you do not necessarily need to if your iOS application will be built entirely on storyboards. You can open the Designer either by double-clicking an existing STORYBOARD file, or right-clicking on a STORYBOARD file and navigating to **Open With | iOS Designer**.

As you can see in the following screenshot, the designer for the iOS interface is made up of five components:

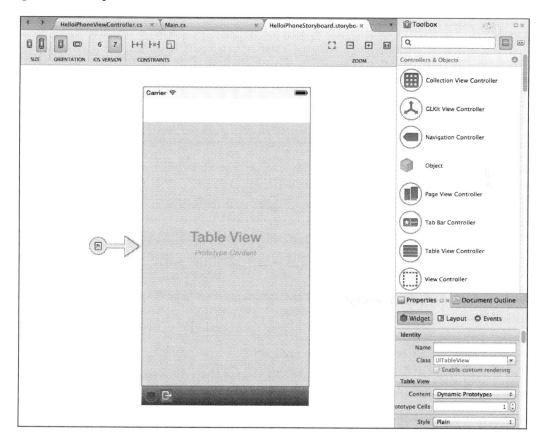

The design surface is your canvas to create new user interfaces, and it will open in the editor area of Xamarin Studio when you open a STORYBOARD file. The **Toolbox** pane shows the controls and objects you can drag-and-drop onto the design surface. The **Properties** box displays information about the currently selected object, such as identity, look, and behavior. The **Document Outline** pad shows a tree representing the layout of your storyboard. You can select a control from the tree and it will be selected in the designer. This is useful to select controls that are deeply nested and difficult or impossible to select using the mouse in the design surface itself.

Finally, the toolbar runs along the top of the design surface, and is broken into five parts:

- **SIZE**: This group lets you choose between 3 and 4 inch screen sizes.
- **ORIENTATION**: This group lets you choose the portrait or landscape orientation view for the open storyboard. Note that this is not an orientation lock, but simply a design reference tool so you can see how your storyboard will be rendered in either orientation.
- **iOS VERSION**: This group lets you choose the iOS version to view the storyboard in. Note that this is not a version lock, but simply a design reference tool so you can see how your storyboard will be rendered in either version of iOS. Be aware that the iOS 6.1 SDK is required to view the storyboard using the iOS 6 button. To install the iOS 6.1 SDK, follow the instructions in *Chapter 1, Installing and Setting Up Xamarin Studio*, under the section titled *iOS simulators*.
- **CONSTRAINTS**: This group lets you add and remove constraints from your objects.
- **ZOOM**: This group lets you zoom in to fit the screen, zoom out, zoom in, and zoom to the actual size.

Creating a storyboard in Xamarin Studio

Let's create a storyboard using the Xamarin Studio designer:

1. Create a new iOS **Empty Project** named `StoryboardDemo`.
2. Add a new **Empty iPhone Storyboard** file to the solution named `MainStoryboard`.
3. Open `MainStoryboard` in the designer.
4. From the **Toolbox** pane, drag a **View Controller** object onto the design surface.
5. Select the **View Controller** object in the design surface.

Chapter 3

6. In the **Properties** box, under the **Identity** heading, there are three fields. Enter `MainStoryboard` into each of them. Once you entered the value in the first field, you will notice that the IDE created the `MainStoryboard.cs` file in the Solution Explorer pad for you.

7. From the **Toolbox** pane under the **Controllers & Objects** group, drag a text field object onto the design surface.

8. In the **Properties** box, under the **Identity** heading, set the **Name** field to `TextField`.

9. From **Toolbox** under the **Controls** group, drag a **Button** object onto the design surface.

10. In the **Properties** box under the **Identity** heading, set the **Name** field to `CopyTextButton`.

11. Also in the **Properties** box, under the **Button** heading, there is a **Title** drop-down combobox. Change the field value below the dropdown to `Copy Text`.

12. Again from **Toolbox** under the **Controllers & Objects** group, drag a **Label** object onto the design surface.

13. In the **Properties** box under the **Identity** field, set the **Name** field to `Label`.

    Your storyboard should look something like what is shown in the following screenshot:

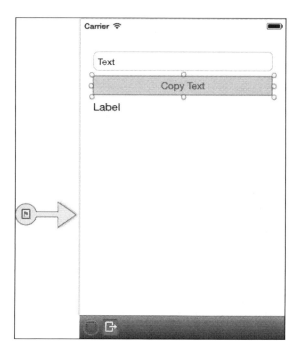

[89]

14. Open the `AppDelegate.cs` file.
15. Replace the class declaration with the following code:

    ```
    public partial class AppDelegate : UIApplicationDelegate
    {
      UIWindow window;
      public static UIStoryboard Storyboard =
        UIStoryboard.FromName ("MainStoryboard", null);
      public static UIViewController initialViewController;

      public override bool FinishedLaunching (UIApplication
        app, NSDictionary options)
      {
        window = new UIWindow (UIScreen.MainScreen.Bounds);

        initialViewController =
          Storyboard.InstantiateInitialViewController () as
            UIViewController;

        window.RootViewController = initialViewController;
        window.MakeKeyAndVisible ();
        return true;
      }
    }
    ```

16. Open the `MainStoryboard.cs` file.
17. Add the following code below the constructor:

    ```
    public override void AwakeFromNib ()
    {
      this.Initialize ();
    }

    public void Initialize()
    {
    }

    public override void ViewDidLoad ()
    {
      base.ViewDidLoad ();

      CopyTextButton.TouchUpInside += (o, e) => {
        Label.Text = TextField.Text;
        TextField.Text = "";
      };
    }
    ```

18. Run the application in the debug mode.

> Occasionally, storyboard projects will fail to build, displaying an error similar to **This class is not key value coding-compliant**. In that case, try to rebuild your project before running it. This will typically resolve the issue and allow you to proceed.
>
> As a side note, you could also add the -f switch to the **Additional mtouch arguments** list (found in the project's options in the **iOS Build** pane). However, this flag will cause the compiler to rebuild your project every time you run it, which can significantly increase your build time as your project grows larger. If you find that you absolutely must rebuild every time you run the app, then the switch will save you some steps. Otherwise, I do not recommend adding the switch.

19. Type some text into the text field, and click the **Copy Text** button. The label should get updated with the text you entered, and the text field should be cleared.

How it works

Once you add the STORYBOARD file to your app, you add an empty `ViewController` object and complete its **Class** and **ID** fields that are critical to the operation of your app. The **Class** field lets you define a custom class to act as the `ViewController` for this pane of the storyboard. The **Storyboard ID** lets you define an ID that you can use to reference this pane in your code. Finally, the **Restoration ID** is used when the `ViewController` needs to be restored to a previous state. Once you enter a value in the **Class** field and tab off, the IDE will automatically create the necessary `ViewController` class if it doesn't already exist. Although it is possible to use an existing class, for now just let the IDE do it for you because the existing classes require some additional setup. Once your `ViewController` object is in place, you added your controls. Giving each control a name allows you to reference that control within your `ViewController` class.

Next, you added code to your `AppDelegate.cs` class. There are two lines of code here that are of particular interest. The first line of code is as follows:

```
public static UIStoryboard Storyboard = UIStoryboard.FromName
    ("MainStoryboard", null);
```

In the preceding line of code, you are registering your storyboard with the AppDelegate by passing the name of the storyboard file.

Working with Xcode and the Android SDK

The second line of code is as follows:

```
initialViewController =
  Storyboard.InstantiateInitialViewController () as
    UIViewController;
```

In the preceding line of code, you are setting and instantiating the initial `ViewController` by calling the `InstantiateInitialViewController()` method of the `UIStoryboard` class.

Finally, in your `MainStoryboard.cs` file you wired up your button to the `TouchUpInside` event handler, as shown in the following code:

```
CopyTextButton.TouchUpInside += (o, e) => {
  Label.Text = TextField.Text;
  TextField.Text = "";
};
```

Android SDK Manager

We have already worked with the **Android SDK Manager** while setting up emulators in *Chapter 1, Installing and Setting Up Xamarin Studio*. At this point, we'll just review the tools in the SDK Manager that we'll be using as Xamarin.Android developers. There are three components you will use on a regular basis, including the **Package Manager**, the **Add-On Sites Manager**, and the **AVD Manager**. The following screenshot shows the package manager:

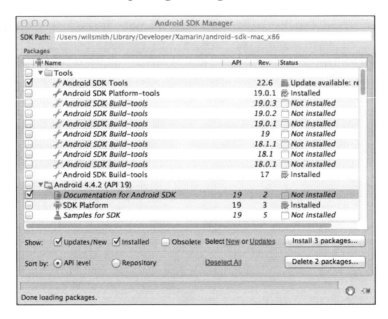

The package manager lets you download and install APIs, tools, documentation, emulator components, as well as other libraries. You can also delete unused or outdated components using this tool as you see fit. Try to avoid the temptation to just download everything at the first sitting though. Some of these components are *very* large so it's best to pick and choose as you need them.

In the following screenshot, you can see the **Add-on Sites Manager**:

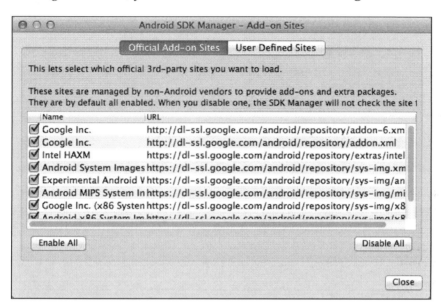

The **Add-on Sites Manager** lets you select both approved and user-defined third-party sites that manage or host additional Android SDK components. Once you have added a site to this list, components and libraries hosted there will appear in the **Package Manager** list for download.

Finally, the following screenshot shows the **AVD Manager**:

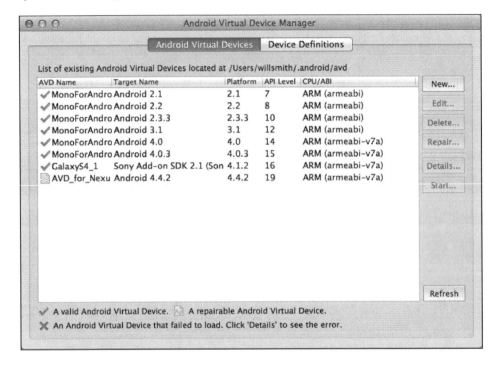

The **AVD Manager** lets you keep track of your emulators. The **Android Virtual Devices** tab tracks the emulators that have already been defined by a user or as part of a downloaded package. The **Device Definitions** tab allows you to track and manage the core definitions that your emulators are based on. For an example of creating a new device and emulator, please refer to the walkthrough in *Chapter 1, Installing and Setting Up Xamarin Studio*.

Android Layouts

Android user interfaces are built using **View** and **ViewGroup** objects. A View is simply an object that draws something on the device's screen that the user can interact with. A ViewGroup is an object that contains other View and ViewGroup objects to define a layout for the interface. A Layout, therefore, is an object that defines the visual structure for a user interface.

The Android framework provides six basic layouts that we can build on. Of course, we can add our own layouts as well. Our applications can programmatically generate and organize objects and manipulate their properties, so we can instantiate our layouts at runtime by defining them in code. We can also declare the user interface elements using XML.

In a typical application, it's common to define your general layout elements using XML, and then modify that layout programmatically at runtime in response to user interaction or application workflow. Therefore, you should become familiar and comfortable with using both of these approaches over time. In general, it's a bad idea to exclusively define your layouts programmatically because doing so tightly binds your presentation layer to your data layer and business logic. Designing your UI in XML keeps the descriptions external to your application code, which means that you can modify or adapt them without the need to recompile. Additionally, defining the layout in XML makes the structure easier to visualize.

Xamarin Studio Designer for Android

Xamarin Studio's Designer for Android will generate layout XML definitions for us. You can open the Designer, shown in the following screenshot, by either double-clicking an existing AXML file, or by adding a new **Android Layout** file to the `/Resources/layout` folder:

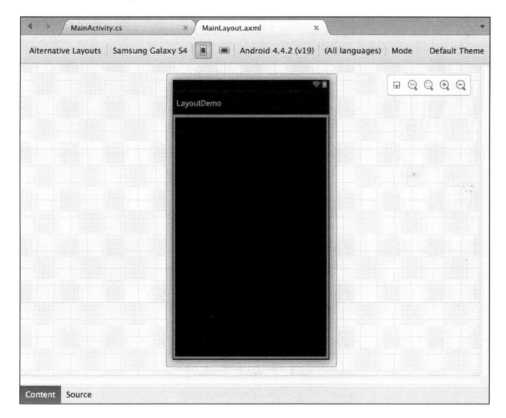

The designer for the Android interface is made up of four components. The design surface is your canvas to create new layouts, and it will open in the editor area of Xamarin Studio when you open an AXML file. The design surface can be viewed in either the content or source mode. The **Toolbox** pane shows the controls and objects you can drag-and-drop onto the design surface. The **Property** pad displays information about the currently selected object, while the **Document Outline** pad shows a tree representing the layout you are currently working with. For more information on these pads please refer to *Chapter 2, Learning and Customizing the XS Environment*.

Creating a Layout in Xamarin Studio

Let's create a Layout using the Xamarin Studio designer:

1. Create a new **Android Application** solution named LayoutDemo.
2. Add a new **Android Layout** file to the /Resources/layouts folder named MainLayout.
3. When the designer opens, open the **Toolbox** pad.
4. From the **Text Fields** group, drag a **Plain Text** object onto your canvas.
5. From the **Form Widgets** group, drag a **Button** object onto your canvas.
6. Again from the **Form Widgets** group, drag a **Text (Medium) label** object onto you canvas.

   Your layout should look something like the following screenshot:

7. Open the `MainActivity.cs` file.
8. Replace the `OnCreate()` method with the following code:
   ```
   protected override void OnCreate (Bundle bundle)
   {
       base.OnCreate (bundle);
       SetContentView (Resource.Layout.MainLayout);

       // Get our button from the layout resource,
       // and attach an event to it
       Button button = FindViewById<Button>
   (Resource.Id.button1);
       TextView textView = FindViewById<TextView>
   (Resource.Id.textView1);
       EditText editText = FindViewById<EditText>
   (Resource.Id.editText1);

       button.Click += delegate {
           textView.Text = editText.Text;
           editText.Text = "";
       };
   }
   ```
9. Run the application in the debug mode.
10. Type some text in the text field, and click the button in the emulator screen. The label should get updated with the text you entered, and the text field should be cleared.

How it works

Looking back at the `MainLayout.axml` file in the designer, notice again the two tabs at the bottom of the designer labeled **Content** and **Source**. Select the **Source** tab and you will see the XML code. This code defines your layout as you have visually designed it, and you can make adjustments here or using the designer. Note the `android:id` attributes, as their values define the name of the object to be rendered by the OS. When you click the **Source** tab, you will see the following code:

```
<?xml version="1.0" encoding="utf-8"?>
<LinearLayout xmlns:android="http://schemas.android.com/apk/res/
android"
    android:orientation="vertical"
    android:layout_width="fill_parent"
    android:layout_height="fill_parent">
    <EditText
```

```
                android:layout_width="match_parent"
                android:layout_height="wrap_content"
                android:id="@+id/editText1" />
        <Button
                android:text="Button"
                android:layout_width="match_parent"
                android:layout_height="wrap_content"
                android:id="@+id/button1" />
        <TextView
                android:text="Medium Text"
                android:textAppearance="?android:attr/textAppearanceMedium"
                android:layout_width="match_parent"
                android:layout_height="41.2dp"
                android:id="@+id/textView1" />
</LinearLayout>
```

In the `MainActivity.OnCreate()` method, you first replace the default code with the following code:

```
SetContentView (Resource.Layout.MainLayout);
```

This code sets the new AXML layout file as the content of the activity you are editing, effectively binding your layout to this activity. Next, you add the following lines:

```
Button button = FindViewById<Button> (Resource.Id.button1);
TextView textView = FindViewById<TextView>
   (Resource.Id.textView1);
EditText editText = FindViewById<EditText>
   (Resource.Id.editText1);
```

These lines of code create local objects that you can manipulate in your code. In each case, an object has been rendered by the OS using the definition in the AXML file, and you then use the generic `FindViewById<T>` to locate and bind to that object by its ID, also defined in the AXML file.

For example, to obtain the instance of the `Button` object, you called `FindViewByID<Button>` because you needed a `Button` object. The `android:id` value of `"@+id/button1"` was converted to `Resource.Id.button1` in your code example. You can use this same convention for objects of any type in your layouts:

```
button.Click += delegate {
    textView.Text = editText.Text;
    editText.Text = "";
};
```

Finally, you are binding to the `Click` event and defining a delegate to handle the event. Within this handler, you are copying the text from the `editText.Text` property into the `textView.Text` property and then clearing the `editText.Text` property.

Summary

In this chapter, we learned about the Xcode IDE and Interface Builder. We learned how to use these tools to create views and view controllers, and how to bind objects in those views to our code behind files in Xamarin Studio. We also discussed the various types of files generated by Xcode and Xamarin Studio when we created these view controllers. Next, we briefly examined the Android SDK Manager and how it is used to create emulators to test our applications. Finally, we examined the Xamarin Studio integrated designer, and created a custom storyboard and layout using this tool.

In the next chapter, we're going to look at the Visual Studio plugin including how to connect to a networked Mac build machine. Following this, we'll examine the various projects, libraries, and file types available for your applications.

4
Plugins, Templates, Libraries, and Files

In this chapter, we will cover the following topics:

- Introduction to the Visual Studio plugin
- Setting up a networked Mac build machine
- Creating an iOS application in Visual Studio
- Project templates
- Libraries
- Files

In this chapter, we will discuss the various components that you can add to your projects. Since some of these components are only available in specific contexts, we first need to discuss the final environmental component—the Visual Studio plugin.

This chapter will focus on a series of walkthroughs to help you set up your build environment to use the Visual Studio plugin. Next, we will discuss the various project templates that can be created inside Xamarin Studio and Visual Studio, with a particular focus on the various library project templates. Finally, we will discuss the types of files you can add to your projects.

Installing the Visual Studio plugin

Xamarin offers a series of plugins to develop iOS and Android applications from within Visual Studio. These plugins allow you to develop apps for iOS, Android, and Windows, all while taking advantage of the tools you're already familiar with. Moreover, you can run Visual Studio inside a **Virtual Machine (VM)** on your Mac, so you don't even need a second development machine.

In order to take advantage of the Visual Studio plugins, you first need a Business or Enterprise subscription to Xamarin as well as a copy of Visual Studio 2010 Professional or higher. For Xamarin.iOS developers, you will also need a networked Mac to act as a build machine because Windows machines can't compile to native iOS code. Additionally, at the time of writing this, whenever you need to work with XIBs you will need to transfer your solution to the Mac and open it from Xamarin.

Since the Visual Studio plugin still requires a Mac for development, you might ask yourself whether there is any advantage of using it. In my opinion, there are several compelling reasons to use the plugin. For one, you're probably already very familiar with the Visual Studio interface and the tools it provides, so using it will increase your productivity. Another advantage is that the plugin allows you to use the full power of Visual Studio, as well as the impressive array of third-party plugins available for that IDE. Lastly, if you intend to write applications that are compatible with Windows devices, the plugin will simplify the development process by allowing you to use one IDE to build the entire suite.

In the following walkthroughs, you will set up a development environment that uses the Visual Studio plugin on a Windows machine or VM. For the purposes of these walkthroughs, we'll assume that you want to develop in iOS and will therefore also want to set up a networked Mac build machine. The process for setting up the Visual Studio plugin using a Windows VM hosted on your Mac is very similar, although the individual mileage might vary.

First, you need to make sure your environment meets the minimum requirements. Your Windows machine will need the following:

- Windows 7 or higher
- Visual Studio 2010 Professional or higher
- Xamarin's plugin for Visual Studio
- Network access to the Mac build machine

Your Mac will need the following:

- OS X Lion or higher
- Xamarin.iOS
- Xcode and the iOS SDK

If you have not already done so, install Xamarin on your Windows and Mac machines, and install Xcode and the iOS SDK on your Mac. For detailed instructions on installing each of these packages, including the Xamarin Unified Installer, please refer to *Chapter 1, Installing and Setting Up Xamarin Studio*.

>
> If you intend to develop apps for Windows Phone 8, you will need **Windows 8 64-bit Pro** or higher because the Windows Phone 8 emulator will not run on Windows 7.
>
> If you intend to develop apps for Windows Phone 8, you will need **Visual Studio 2012 Professional** or higher.

Configuring your Mac

To configure your Mac, perform the following steps:

1. From the **Apple** menu, open **System Preferences**.
2. Open the **Personal** group.
3. Select the **Security and Privacy** item.
4. Open the **Firewall** tab, and ensure the Firewall is turned off.

Configuring your Windows machine

If you haven't configured your Windows machine already, download and install the Xamarin Unified Installer. This installer includes a tool called **Xamarin Bonjour Service**, which runs Apple's network discovery protocol. Xamarin Bonjour Service requires administrator rights, so you may want to just run the installer as an administrator.

Configuring a Windows VM within Mac

There is really no difference between using the Visual Studio plugin from a Windows machine or from a VM using software, such as Parallels or VMware. However, if you are running Xamarin Studio on a Retina Macbook Pro, it is advisable to adjust the hardware video settings. Otherwise, some of the elements within Xamarin Studio will render poorly making them difficult to use. The following screenshot contains the recommended video settings:

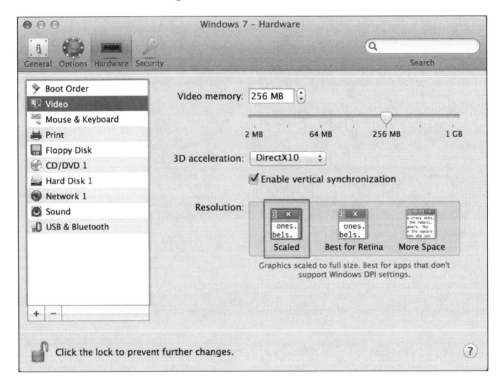

To adjust the settings in Parallels, follow these steps:

1. If your Windows VM is running, shut it down.
2. With your VM shut down, go to **Virtual Machine | Configure…**.
3. Choose the **Hardware** tab.
4. Select the **Video** group.
5. Under **Resolution**, choose **Scaled**.

Final installation steps

Now that the necessary tools are installed and the settings have been enabled, you still need to link to your Xamarin account in Visual Studio, as well as connect Visual Studio to your Mac build machine. To connect to your Xamarin account, follow these steps:

1. In Visual Studio, go to **Tools** | **Xamarin Account...**.
2. Click **Login to your Xamarin Account** and enter your credentials.
3. Once your credentials are verified, you will receive a confirmation message.

To connect to your Mac build machine, follow these steps:

1. On your Mac, open **Spotlight** and type `Xamarin build host`.
2. Choose **Xamarin.iOS Build Host** under the **Applications** results group.
3. After the **Build Host** utility dialog opens click the **Pair** button to continue.
4. You will be provided with a PIN. Write this down.
5. On your PC, open Xamarin Studio.
6. Go to **Tools** | **Options** | **Xamarin** | **iOS Settings**.
7. After the **Build Host utility** opens, click the **Continue** button.
8. If your Mac and network are correctly configured, you will see your Mac in the list of available build machines.
9. Choose your build machine and click the **Continue** button.
10. You will be prompted to enter the PIN. Do so, then click the **Pair** button.
11. Once the machines are paired, you can build, test, and deploy applications using the networked Mac.

If for whatever reason you want to unpair these two machines, open the Xamarin. iOS Build Host on your Mac again, and click the **Invalidate PIN** button. When prompted, complete the process by clicking the **Unpair** button.

Configuring the Visual Studio toolbar

It's a good idea to configure your Visual Studio toolbars so that the Xamarin plugin can be easily accessed. To configure the toolbar in Visual Studio 2010 Professional, follow these steps:

1. Right-click the **Standard** toolbar and choose **Customize...** from the menu.
2. Select the **Commands** tab.
3. Select the **Toolbar** radio button.

4. Select the **Standard** toolbar from the drop-down list of options.
5. Select the **Solution Configurations** widget from the **Controls** window.
6. Click the **Add command...** button.
7. Under the **Categories** list, choose the **Build** category.
8. In the **Commands** window, choose the **Solution Platforms** command.
9. Click the **OK** button.
10. Click the **Close** button.

Setting up the toolbar under Visual Studio 2013 Professional is slightly easier:

1. Click the menu drop-down button to the right of the **Standard** toolbar.
2. Choose the **Add or Remove Buttons** group from the menu.
3. Select the **Solution Platforms** option from the list provided.

Creating an iPhone application in Visual Studio

The process of creating an iPhone application in Visual Studio is very similar to that of Xamarin Studio. In this walkthrough, you will create a new application that will consist entirely of code. You will not be adding XIBs or storyboards and you will define your views programmatically by performing the following steps:

1. Open Visual Studio and create a new **iOS** solution using the **iPhone Empty Project** template.
2. Name your project `Visual Studio iOS Demo` and click the **OK** button.
3. Add a new **Empty class** to your project.
4. Name the class `MyRootViewController`.
5. Add a `using` statement for the MonoTouch.UIKit framework, as shown in the following line of code:

   ```
   Using MonoTouch.UIKit;
   ```

6. Set the class to inherit from `UIViewController`, as shown in the following code:

   ```
   classMyRootViewController : UIViewController
   {
   }
   ```

7. Override the `ViewDidLoad()` method:

   ```
   public override void ViewDidLoad()
   {
   base.ViewDidLoad();
   View.BackgroundColor = UIColor.LightGray;
   }
   ```

8. Open the `AppDelegate.cs` file.

9. Just before the `FinishedLaunching()` method, add the following code:

   ```
   MyRootViewControllerrootVC = new MyRootViewController();
   UINavigationControllernavigationController = new
     UINavigationController();
   ```

10. Replace the default code in the `FinishedLaunching()` method with the following code:

    ```
    window = new UIWindow(UIScreen.MainScreen.Bounds);

    rootVC.Title = "My Controller";

    window.RootViewController = navigationController;
    navigationController.PushViewController (rootVC, true);
    this.window.MakeKeyAndVisible ();
    return true;
    ```

You have now created a new custom view controller and set that as the root view controller in your application. When you run the app at this stage, you should see a completely gray screen on your simulator or device and a header with the title **My Controller**, but not much else. Let's continue by adding some controls to your new custom view:

1. Back in the `MyRootViewController` file, add a `using` statement for `System.Drawing`, shown here:

   ```
   Using System.Drawing;
   ```

2. Now in the `ViewDidLoad()` method, add the following lines of code:

   ```
   float h = 31.0f;
   float w = View.Bounds.Width;

   UITextFieldtextField = new UITextField
   {
       Placeholder = "Enter some text",
   BorderStyle = UITextBorderStyle.RoundedRect,
   ```

```
        Frame = new RectangleF(10, 75, w - 20, h)
};

UILabel label = new UILabel
{
    Frame = new RectangleF(10, 120, w - 20, h)
};

UIButtonsubmitButton =
    UIButton.FromType(UIButtonType.RoundedRect);
submitButton.Frame = new RectangleF(10, 170, w - 20, 44);
submitButton.SetTitle("Submit", UIControlState.Normal);
submitButton.TouchUpInside += delegate
{
label.Text = textField.Text;
textField.Text = "":
};

View.AddSubview(textField);
View.AddSubview(submitButton);
View.AddSubview(label);
```

If you run your application at this stage, you will see a view that looks something like the following screenshot:

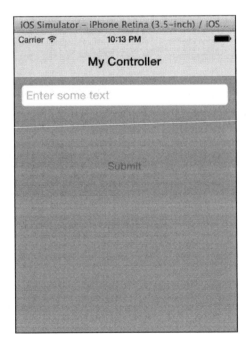

The app now has duplicate functionality to the app you created in *Chapter 3, Working with Xcode and the Android SDK*, using Xamarin Studio and Xcode as your design platform. As you can see, there is a little more code involved and you need to manually define the location and size of each control, but it's really not too complicated.

How it works

First, you set up the basic framework of your new application. You began by creating a new view controller by inheriting from the `UIViewController` class. Next, you created an override of the `UIViewController.ViewDidLoad()` method and you used that to change the background color property of the view. Finally, you tied your new customer view controller into your application using the `AppDelegate` class. Your code initializes an instance of the `MyRootViewController` class and then initializes an instance of `UINavigationController` (both outside of the `FinishedLaunching()` method for garbage collection purposes). Then, you set the navigation controller instance as the root view controller of your app. The window object is, effectively, your application container, while you can think of the root view controller as your home screen.

Note that a navigation controller is a container for other views and is itself treated like a view in this context. The navigation controller is responsible for maintaining a stack of memory that keeps track of which view is currently visible, plus any views that exist underneath the visible view. Views are pushed and popped on and off the stack using the `PushViewController()` and `PopViewControllerAnimated()` methods. Your application can have multiple navigation controllers, but keeping that number to a minimum makes it easier to maintain your app (and your sanity).

> Be aware that every time you create a new view, you are allocating a chunk of precious system memory to maintain that view. Once you push that view onto the stack, its memory will remain allocated until the view is popped. For this reason, it is very important from a development point of view to maintain a clear path of navigation throughout your app, and avoid circular navigational paths. This kind of design flaw can result in unused views hanging around in memory, causing seemingly random out-of-memory exceptions that can be extremely difficult to diagnose.

Once your application framework was established, you created three controls programmatically. Note that each of your controls, like every object in a view, has a `Frame` property. In iOS, `Frame` defines an object's location in the parent view and the object's size. In your code, you are defining the frame object for each of your controls using a `RectangleF` object in the format `RectangleF(xCoordinate, yCoordinate, width, height)`, where each of the parameters is a `float` data type.

Project templates

Xamarin Studio comes bundled with a number of project templates. In this section, we'll examine the most commonly used template options provided for Xamarin.iOS, Xamarin.Android, and Xamarin.Mac. There are several advanced project templates that won't be covered in this text. In addition, there are several commonly used project templates for mobile apps, but these will be discussed in detail in *Chapter 5, Working with Xamarin.Forms*.

iOS project templates

Xamarin Studio provides several iOS project templates for you to choose from. These templates are organized into groups by platforms, namely iPhone, iPad, and Universal. Any project template that you can create in Visual Studio is the same as its counterpart in Xamarin Studio. As previously mentioned, you cannot add XIBs to your projects in Visual Studio so your template options are slightly limited while using the plugin. You can still build views and view controllers programmatically, plus you can add storyboards, but if you want to add XIBs, you will need to open your project in Xamarin Studio on a Mac and add them there. Here's a list of the available project types for iOS:

- **Empty Project**: This is a simple iOS application frame that includes only the `AppDelegate.cs`, `Info.plist` and `Main.cs` files. This project template is not available in the storyboard format, but it is available using the Visual Studio plugin. This project type is available in both C# and F#.

- **Single View Application**: This includes all of the files from the **Empty Project**, plus a single XIB file prewired to the `AppDelegate` class. The single view template is available to all of the iOS project groups, as well as the Visual Studio plugin, although you can't edit the XIB file using Visual Studio. This project type is available in both C# and F#.

- **iOS Tabbed Application**: This uses a tab navigation UI design. This UI is built using the `UITabBarController` class. The tabbed-application template will create a project framework to create tabbed applications. This template is available to all of the iOS project groups, as well as the Visual Studio plugin. This project type is currently only available in C#.

- **iOS Utility Application**: This template will create the framework for a utility application. Utility applications are fairly simple, consisting of one main view and one supporting view, which are presented by means of a flip animation. These applications are optimized for simple tasks that require very little user interaction. At the time of writing this, the utility application template is available for the iPad, iPhone, and Universal groups, but it is not available using the Visual Studio plugin. This project type is currently only available in C#.

- **Page Based Application**: This template will create a framework for a page-based application. Page-based applications use `UIPageViewController`, which changes views while swiping, and uses an animation transition resembling a page being turned into a book. The page-based application template is only available in the iPad, iPhone, and Universal iOS groups, and it is not available using the Visual Studio plugin. This project type is currently only available in C#.

- **Web View Application**: This simply uses the `UIWebView` control to display a web page. The **Web View Application** template creates a framework, which includes a view based on web view control. This template is only available in the iPad, iPhone, and Universal iOS groups, and is not available using the Visual Studio plugin. This project type is currently only available in C#.

- **Sprite-Kit Application**: Use this template if you are into game development. Sprite Kit is Apple's native game framework in order to render 2D graphics and animation. It includes support for many of the functions you would expect to find in a game engine, such as animations, collision detection, A/V support, and more. The Sprite-Kit Application template is only available in the iPad, iPhone, and Universal iOS groups, and is not available using the Visual Studio plugin. This project type is currently only available in C#.

> For more information about Sprite Kit, please review this article from Apple at `https://developer.apple.com/Library/ios/documentation/GraphicsAnimation/Conceptual/SpriteKit_PG/Introduction/Introduction.html`.

- **Master-Detail Application**: This template utilizes the **Split View Controller** design. The Master-Detail Application template is available to all of the iOS project groups, as well as the Visual Studio plugin. This project type is currently only available in C#.

- **iOS Binding Project**: This allows you to consume third-party Objective-C libraries for use within Xamarin Studio. This project uses the same tools that Xamarin uses to bring the native iOS APIs into Xamarin Studio. Note that if you need to consume standard C libraries, you should just use the **P/Invoke framework** already built into .NET. More details on the binding project type will be discussed later in the *Libraries* section of this chapter. The **iOS Binding Project** template is found under the main iOS group, but it is not available using the Visual Studio plugin. This project type is currently only available in C#.

- **iOS Unit Tests Project**: This template will create a unit test project based on the Touch.Unit framework, which includes an iOS test component as well as a modified version of NUnitLite. The iOS Unit Test Project template is found under the main iOS group, but it is not available using the Visual Studio plugin. This project type is currently only available in C#.
- **iOS Library Project**: This template will allow you to create packages of files that can be shared between solutions. These packages can contain the actual files or links to those files. More details on the Library project type and file linking will be discussed later in the *Libraries* section of this chapter. The **iOS Library Project** template is found under the main iOS group, but it is not available using the Visual Studio plugin. This project type is currently only available in C#.
- **OpenGL Application**: This template allows you to create apps that utilize the OpenGL framework. The **OpenGL Application** template is available to all of the iOS project groups, as well as the Visual Studio plugin. This project type is currently only available in C#.

What are iPhone, iPad, and Universal applications?

From a development perspective, iPhone and iPad applications are fairly similar. You'll use the same tools to build them, the same code for the most part, as well as many of the same controls. From a design perspective, however, iPhone and iPad applications are quite different. The additional real estate available on an iPad means that views can contain more controls and functionality. Plus, the iPad itself introduces additional UI controls and features that target the larger screen space.

These changes can positively affect user experience and the overall workflow in the application if you take advantage of them. One way to do this is to create separate views targeting iPhones and iPads. As you can imagine, this means you could potentially double the amount of work you need to put into developing and maintaining your UI.

Alternatively, you can create a **Universal** application. Universal applications are optimized to run on iPhones, iPads, and even the newer iPad Mini devices, and provide the best experience for the user. Customizing the views for each type of device will still require some additional tweaking on your part, but not nearly the workload needed to create and maintain dual UIs.

Android project templates

Xamarin Studio provides eight Android project templates for you to choose from. Most of these templates are available from within Visual Studio, with the exception of the Unit Test and Web View templates. Again, each of the project templates available in Visual Studio is the same as its Xamarin Studio counterpart:

- **Android Application**: This is a blank Android framework that you can build on. When you create a project using this template, it will include `<solution>` and `<project>` of the same name, folders for `Assets`, `Resources`, and `Properties`, and a `MainActivity.cs` file. This project type is available in both C# and F#.

- **Android Honeycomb**: This project template will create an application that supports the Android 3.x operating system and above. This application will not provide support for features from API Level 14 and above. However, some backward compatibility for Android 1.6 (API Level 4) through Android 2.3.3 (API level 10 — Gingerbread) can be introduced using the Android Support Package. This project type is available in both C# and F#.

> For more information on the Android Support Package, please refer to the documentation at `http://developer.android.com/tools/support-library/index.html` and `http://docs.xamarin.com/guides/android/platform_features/fragments/part_4_-_providing_backwards_compatibility_with_the_android_support_package/`.

- **Android Ice Cream Sandwich**: This project template will create an application that supports the Android 4.0 and 4.0.3 operating system. This project template does not automatically include support for Android 4.1 (API level 16 — Jelly Bean) or above. However, it is possible to add additional features for Android 4.1 and Android 4.4 (API Level 19 — KitKat). For Jelly Bean support, you must run Xamarin.Android 4.2.6 or higher and have Android 4.1 (API Level 16) installed. For KitKat support, you must run Xamarin.Android 4.11.0 or higher and have Android 4.3 (API Level 19) installed. This project type is available in both C# and F#.

- **Android Library**: This is a package of source code and Android resources that can be shared between multiple Android projects. As with its iOS counterpart, this library contains the actual files or links to those files. This project type is available in both C# and F#.
- **Java Bindings Library**: This project template creates a .NET assembly containing the necessary Managed Callable Wrappers classes, JAR files, and resources for Android Library projects embedded into it. By referencing this assembly, a Xamarin.Android project may use an existing third-party Java library. More details on the binding project types will be discussed later in the *Libraries* section of this chapter. This project type is currently only available in C#.

> For more information on building and using Java Bindings Library projects to import third-party Android libraries, please refer to http://docs.xamarin.com/guides/android/advanced_topics/java_integration_overview/binding_a_java_library_(.jar)/.

- **Android WebView**: This template will create an application project that can display web pages using the WebView control. This project type is currently only available in C#.
- **Android Unit Test**: This project template will create a unit test project targeting an Android application. This project type is available in both C# and F#.
- **Android OpenGL Application**: This template is similar to its iOS counterpart in that it creates a framework in order to work with graphics in your applications. This project type is available in both C# and F#.

Mac and Mac (open source) project templates

For the sake of completeness, we will also discuss the project types available through **Xamarin.Mac**. There are two main groups of projects in this package: **Mac** and **Mac (open source)**. The main difference between the **Mac** and the **Mac (open source)** options is that the latter utilizes a more limited set of APIs.

- **Xamarin.Mac**: This project template creates a single-window Mac project that you can build on as needed. Under the open source group, this is referred to as a **MonoMac** project. This project type is available in both C# and F#.

- **Xamarin.Mac Library**: This project is a package of source code and Mac resources that can be shared between multiple projects. As with its iOS and Android siblings, this library can contain the actual files or links to those files. The open source version is called **MonoMac Library**. This project type is currently only available in C#.
- **Empty Xamarin.Mac**: This project is a blank slate for you to build on. Its open source counterpart is the **Empty MonoMac** project. This project type is available in both C# and F#.
- **Xamarin.Mac Document**: This project template lets you create an Apple Document application. Document-based apps organize multiple documents, each within its own window, often displaying multiple documents simultaneously. The open source version is called **MonoMac Document**. This project type is currently only available in C#.

Libraries

There are two project templates that need to be explored in more detail due to the power they provide to your applications. These are the **Portable Class Library** (PCL) and the **Binding Library** projects.

Portable Class Library

Developing true cross-platform applications would not be feasible without a significant amount of code sharing. Unfortunately, each platform is built to a different .NET Core Library Profile. This means you can't directly share code libraries between different platform solutions because each of these libraries is built to target unique profiles. There are three ways to work around this problem.

The first is to simply duplicate code across your projects. Maintaining multiple sets of duplicate code is tedious and prone to errors such as copy/paste fail. Duplicate code means you end up with multiple separate solutions instead of a cross-platform application. If code duplication was the only option it would be better to just write your applications in native than to incur the costs of so much additional development and maintenance overhead.

The second option is to implement file linking. File linking uses symbolic links for a set of files, rather than importing the files themselves. This means you can edit these files in one solution, and see the changes in each of the solutions that link to these files.

The final option is to use PCL. With PCL, you can write code and create libraries that can then be shared in multiple platforms including iOS, Android, and Windows Phone. The **Portable Library** project template can be found under the C# group and is available in both Xamarin Studio as well as Visual Studio.

> Both the file linking and PCL approaches have their strengths and weaknesses. For instance, file linking can introduce an additional build step if you are building reusable components that are intended for external use only, while PCLs require some extra work to separate profile specific code into targeted libraries. For a more detailed discussion on when to choose file linking or the PCL approach, please review http://docs.xamarin.com/guides/cross-platform/application_fundamentals/building_cross_platform_applications/sharing_code_options/.

Binding Project

The second library project we need to explore is the **Binding project** template. The importance and value of this project type cannot be overstated, as it is one of those areas where Xamarin Studio really shines. When working on iOS or Android projects, you will frequently find ideas from third-party libraries and SDKs that you want to incorporate into your own application. For these cases, you can either recreate the functionality from scratch, or use binding projects to create a C# wrapper for the native third-party library.

iOS Binding Project

The iOS Binding Project template uses the same tools that Xamarin uses to wrap the iOS APIs with C#. When you create a new iOS Binding Project, it will contain an `ApiDefinition.cs` file and a `StructsAndEnums.cs` file. The `ApiDefinition.cs` file will contain the API contract definition, while the `StructsAndEnums.cs` file will contain any definitions required by your code.

Creating a comprehensive, high-quality binding takes time, but luckily there is a new tool called **Objective Sharpie** that can help generate the API contract for you. Objective Sharpie works by parsing the header files of the native library you are trying to import, and mapping the public API to the binding definition. At the time of writing this, Objective Sharpie is a standalone Mac OS X application but there are plans to integrate it into Xamarin Studio at some point in the future. This tool will not eliminate all of the work needed to create the contract, but it will greatly reduce the effort required.

> For more information on using Objective Sharpie, please review the Xamarin documentation at `http://developer.xamarin.com/guides/ios/advanced_topics/binding_objective-c/objective_sharpie/`.

Java Bindings Library

If you want to include third-party Java libraries with your application, you have two choices. You can either use the **Java Native Interface (JNI)** to invoke calls to the libraries directly, or you can create a Java Bindings Library project to wrap the library in C#. The Java Bindings Library project actually uses a JNI bridge called Managed Callable Wrappers to implement the bindings. Although the process of creating the wrapper is not completely automated yet, it's still much easier to use an existing Android library within a Java Bindings Library project than it is to write your own for a specific function or feature.

Files

Many of the file types you can add to your projects in Xamarin Studio are self-explanatory for developers, but it doesn't hurt to review some of those that are unique to Xamarin Studio, as well as those that are platform-specific. Unfortunately, detailed demonstrations of how to use each of these files is beyond the scope of this book. Hopefully, these descriptions can spark your imagination and provide ideas for your applications:

- Native iOS and Android applications can support hybrid HTML 5 functionality by using the **Razor templating engine**. Adding a **Preprocessed Razor Template** file to your project will allow you to incorporate Razor-powered web apps into your application.

- Add an **Asset Catalog** to your iOS 7 application to help simplify management of the various images needed for the user interface of your application. An **Asset Catalog** is not a simple resource file. When you add this object to your project, it will create a folder called `Images.xcassets`, and within that two more folders called `AppIcons.appiconset` and `LaunchImages.launchimage`. Within each of these folders there is a `Contents.json` file, which is a form of visual designer for your image collection, as shown in the following screenshot:

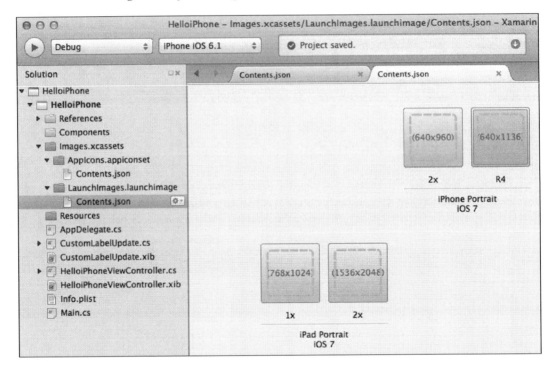

- Within the `Contents.json` file, your images are organized into groups called sets, each based on an iOS version and device type. These sets include a tile representing the dimension definitions required by your application for each image resource. With this designer open, you can drag-and-drop images into their respective tiles to assign them as needed throughout your app. Finally, if you need additional image groups, you can add new subfolders to the `Images.xcassets` folder and Xamarin Studio will automatically include a new `Contents.json` file in that folder.

- An interface definition is simply an **Interface Builder** (**IB**) file. You can add a new IB file to your iPhone or iPad application by selecting the respective **Empty Interface Definition** file type. This new file is a completely blank canvas to design views for your application.

- A storyboard is a hybrid user interface model that includes both the view controllers and the navigation mechanisms in one file. You can add a blank storyboard to your iPhone and iPad applications by selecting the **Empty iPhone Storyboard** or **Empty iPad Storyboard** file, respectively.

- A view inherits from the iOS UIView class, and it is the foremost way an iOS application will interact with a user. It defines a rectangular area with dimensions specific to the device it is running on. This definition also includes the content management for objects in that area. Views can contain zero or more subviews, and it has the ability to define the size and position of these subviews as needed. Views are themselves responders that can handle touch events. You can add a view to your iPhone or iPad application by choosing the **iPhone View** or **iPad View** file type, respectively.

- A view controller is the fundamental view-management model for all iOS applications, inheriting from the UIViewController class. They manage sets of views, coordinating its work with other model objects so your app presents a unified user experience. You can add a view controller to your iPhone, iPad, or Universal application by choosing the **iPhone View Controller**, **iPad View Controller**, and **Universal View Controller** files, respectively.

- Table view controllers are controller objects that manage an instance of UITableView. This object inherits from the iOS UITableViewController class. You can add table view controllers to your iPhone or iPad application by choosing the **iPhone Table View Controller** or **iPad Table View Controller** files, respectively.

- Table view cells inherit from the iOS UITableViewCell class. They define the attributes and behaviors of a cell that appears within the view bounds of a table view. You can add an instance of this control to your iPhone, iPad, or Universal application by choosing the respective file type.

- Collection view controllers are view controllers that consist of a collection view, and they inherit from the iOS UICollectionViewController class. You can add an instance of this control to your application using the **iOS Collection View Controller**.

- Collection view cells inherit from the iOS UICollectionViewCell class. These objects represent the content of a single data item while that item is visible within the bounds of the parent view, and they can be customized as needed. You can add a new collection view cell to your iPhone, iPad, or Universal application by choosing the respective file type.

- A **Dialog View Controller (DVC)** inherits from and provides a simplified API to the iOS UITableViewController class. The control is essentially a view that contains a table view.

> For more information on any of the above iOS control types, please review the Apple Developer library at `https://developer.apple.com/`.

- A **property list (PList)** file is a special XML file used by iOS applications to store data for the application, which will change frequently. This file stores the data outside of the main app bundle so any changes will not require the application to be rebuilt. You can think of the Plist file as being similar to a `config` file in .NET applications.

- A settings bundle file has the name `Settings.bundle` and resides in the top level directory of your solution. Settings bundles are used by **Settings App Interface** to implement a set of pages to navigate the application's settings.

- An **Android Activity** at its simplest form is a screen in an Android application. Since Android's architecture doesn't rely on a single application instance, an application can be seen as a conglomeration of one or more activities. If you are new to Android, it will be important to understand the concept of an activity as it might be the most important concept in Android development.

- Use the **Android Fragment** file type to add a new fragment to your application. Unlike the iOS platform, which serves a very finite number of device types, Android can run on more devices and in more shapes and sizes than I can think of. As of Android 3.0, the concept of the Fragment was introduced to help service flexible user interface designs for the many screen sizes found on modern devices. You can think of a Fragment as a user interface module that can be mixed and matched with other modules to assemble screens that are aesthetically pleasing and contain a logical workflow, even on very different devices. What's really great about fragments is that the developer doesn't have to lay out the various modules to work with every screen size—you just need to provide the fragments and the activity will decide which fragments to use automatically!

- An **Android Layout** will add a new layout to your application. For more information on layouts, please refer to *Chapter 3, Working with Xcode and the Android SDK*.

- An **Android View** will add a new view to your application. For more information on views, please refer to *Chapter 3, Working with Xcode and the Android SDK*.

- In order for your Android application to work with remote notifications, you must configure a **Broadcast Receiver** to listen for the intents that the **Google Services Framework** will publish when it receives a message from the **Google Cloud Messaging** service.

> For more information on using the Google Services Framework and Google Cloud Messaging in Xamarin.Android projects, refer to Xamarin's documentation on how to implement these features at http://developer.xamarin.com/guides/cross-platform/application_fundamentals/notifications/android/remote_notifications_in_android/.

Summary

In this chapter, we learned about the Visual Studio plugin, and walked through setting up plugin, as well as binding Visual Studio to a networked Mac build machine. We discussed each of the major project templates available in Xamarin Studio, pointing out to the ones that are available when using the Visual Studio plugin. We also looked at the various library types and how they can be leveraged to reduce your development workload. Finally, we briefly examined the file types available to use in your solutions.

In the next chapter, we will take a look at the Xamarin.Forms framework newly introduced by Xamarin 3. You will learn to build a fully functional cross-platform application in just a few minutes using XAML and the UI design API included with the framework.

Working with Xamarin.Forms

In this chapter, we will cover the following topics:

- Requirements for using Xamarin.Forms
- The Xamarin.Forms project templates
- The Xamarin.Forms components
- The API design
- The XAML design

In addition to the new iOS designer, Xamarin 3 introduces another powerful toolset to Xamarin Studio: the Xamarin.Forms framework. Xamarin.Forms is a UI toolkit abstraction that allows developers to rapidly create user interfaces that will run natively on iOS, Android, and Windows Phone devices all from within the same solution.

This works because the Xamarin.Forms toolkit is a wrapper that sits on top of the native UI elements from each platform. At compile time, the UI elements you create in these projects are converted to their native counterparts. This means that your application will retain the look and feel of a native application across all three platforms.

This chapter will briefly introduce the project templates available in the Xamarin.Forms framework, and you will learn to use those templates to create a solution that will run on iOS and Android devices using a single code base.

Requirements for using Xamarin.Forms

Technically speaking, Xamarin.Forms is loaded with the Starter edition of Xamarin Studio. Unfortunately, the compiled applications are roughly 512 KB (iOS) and 768 KB (Android) at a minimum, which exceeds the compiled application size limit of 64 KB imposed on the Starter edition of Xamarin Studio. As a result, you will need to obtain an **Indie** license or higher for either Xamarin.iOS or Xamarin.Android to build apps using Xamarin.Forms.

If you would like to try out Xamarin.Forms but you don't want to make that financial commitment yet, you can get a fully functional trial subscription for both Xamarin. iOS and Xamarin.Android. Although this trial only lasts for 30 days, it will provide you with more than enough time to follow the walkthroughs later in this chapter.

> If your trial period is over, you might be able to get a one-time extension for the purpose of test driving the Xamarin.Forms framework by sending e-mail to `hello@xamarin.com` and making a polite request. As far as I know, this extension is granted to interested developers as a courtesy from Xamarin. This courtesy is not part of any official policy I am aware of, though, so there are no guarantees it will be granted.

The Xamarin.Forms project templates

Xamarin.Forms introduces three additional project templates for you to choose from. At the time of writing this, these templates are only available in C# format:

- **Blank App (Xamarin.Forms Portable)**: This template will create a blank application based on PCL. In *Chapter 4*, *Plugins, Templates, Libraries, and Files*, we learned that PCL allows you to share code across multiple platforms and any refactoring will update all references. PCL, however, lacks support for preprocessor directives, and only a subset of .NET functions are available.
- **Blank App (Xamarin.Forms Shared)**: This template will create a blank application based on the shared project paradigm. Shared projects can utilize preprocessor directives and can contain platform-specific references while remaining usable across all platforms. Although shared projects have no output type, that's not a problem in this context since the solution must also contain a platform-specific project for whichever platform you are targeting.
- **Class Library (Xamarin.Forms Portable)**: This template will allow you to create a standard class library project that can be shared across all Xamarin. Forms applications.

The components of Xamarin.Forms

The goal of Xamarin.Forms is to enable individuals or teams to rapidly develop cross-platform apps, primarily targeting enterprise use. In my opinion, this goal has been achieved because creating cross-platform applications using Xamarin.Forms is remarkably simple. There are three primary skills that you need to become familiar with to get started: data binding, the Xamarin.Forms components, and navigation in Xamarin.Forms.

Data binding

Data binding is a process that establishes a read/write connection between UI components and the business logic of an application. Typically, bindings can be established as either one-way or two-way data binding. In one-way data binding, changes in the source will update the target or changes in the target will update the source. In two-way data binding, changes in either the source or target will update the other.

Anyone who has built an app using the MVVM design paradigm should be very familiar with the concept and power provided by data binding. Personally, I didn't appreciate how powerful it was until I had to build native iOS applications and learned that data binding is not a built-in component of every language.

Luckily, the Xamarin.Forms framework includes the `BindableObjects` class, which implements the data binding infrastructure in a way that will feel familiar to WPF and Silverlight developers. This infrastructure includes support for both one- and two-way binding, value converters, static resources, ItemsSource, and data templates. The `INotifyPropertyChanged` and `INotifyCollectionChanged` interfaces are included, although there is no `INotifyDataErrorInfo` implementation this time. Also, binding validation is missing (at the time of writing this), but you can easily work around that limitation by implementing your own entry-point validation.

Components

Having the ability to create boilerplate UI components that will run on multiple platforms and can be compiled using native controls is extremely useful. Xamarin.Forms goes a step further, however, giving you the ability to tailor components per platform by writing custom renderers. This means that your designs are not limited to the basic controls currently available; you can customize how the controls appear and these customizations can be unique for each platform.

Xamarin.Forms provides four primary core components that you can use to create your applications:

- **View**: This component represents base user controls in Xamarin.Studio. Controls such as labels, buttons, and textboxes are all examples of Views.
- **Page**: This component represents `ViewController` in iOS, an Activity in Android, and a Page in Windows Phone.
- **Layout**: Layouts are View containers used to organize sublayouts and Views. Typical examples of Layouts include the Grid and StackLayout controls. Layouts will normally contain logic used for organizing their child components.
- **Cell**: This is a simplified element that defines how list and table items are rendered and displayed. This option allows you to combine a label with other visual elements in lists and tables.

Navigation

In a Xamarin.Forms application, your in-memory Pages are stored in a stack data structure, with the topmost Page being the one that is visible to the user. For navigation, Pages need to be pushed and popped on and off this stack as the user navigates through the application. In this respect, navigation of Xamarin.Forms somewhat resembles that of iOS applications; except in the case of Xamarin.Forms, navigation is handled using asynchronous calls.

These asynchronous calls are defined in the `INavigation` interface, and each call returns a `Task` object that can be used to check whether or not the navigation was successful. The `NavigationPage` class is included in the framework, and it is similar to `UINavigationController` of iOS. The `NavigationPage` class implements `INavigation`, and acts as a Page manager, neatly providing a container and mechanism to push and pop Pages when the application executes.

The API design

As mentioned earlier, there are two ways to build apps using Xamarin.Forms. The first method is to use the built-in user interface API methods. This approach is strictly code-based; if you're comfortable using code to create all of your Pages, then this is the way to go. Another way is to use XAML to design your Pages, which will be discussed later in this chapter.

Since I'm writing this chapter at the height of the spring fishing season, I would like to build an app that can help my fellow anglers in some small way. Let's demonstrate building a Xamarin.Forms application that lists types of fishing hooks and provides brief details on their selection and use for various game fishing species. First, we'll set up the solution by performing the following steps:

1. In Xamarin Studio, create a new solution. Choose the **Blank App (Xamarin.Forms Portable)** project template by navigating to **C# | Mobile Apps**, as shown in the following screenshot:

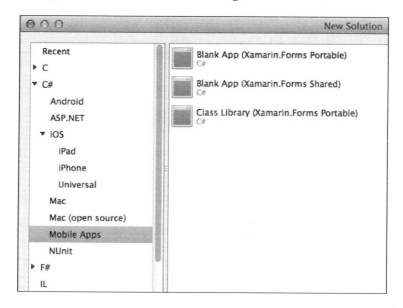

2. Name your project `FishHooksAPI` and click the **OK** button.
3. Your solution will open and the Solution Explorer will display three projects, including `FishHooksAPI`, `FishHooksAPI.Android`, and `FishHooksAPI.iOS`.
4. Add three new folders named `Models`, `ViewModels`, and `Views` to the `FishHooksAPI` project.
5. Right-click the `Models` folder and choose **New File** under **Add**.
6. Choose the **Empty Class** file type from **General**.
7. Name your file `FishHook` and click the **OK** button.
8. Right-click the `ViewModels` folder and choose **New File** under **Add**.
9. Choose the **General | Empty Class** file type.
10. Name your file `FishHooksViewModel` and click the **OK** button.
11. Right-click the `Views` folder and choose **New File** under **Add**.

12. Choose the **General | Empty Class** file type.
13. Name your file `FishHooksPage` and click the **OK** button.
14. Right-click the `Views` folder and choose **New File** under **Add**.
15. Choose the **Empty Class** file type under **General**.
16. Name your file `FishHookDetails` and click the **OK** button.

    Your solution should now look like the following screenshot:

    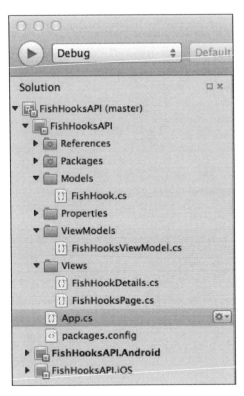

Next, you'll add the classes to your project:

1. Open the `FishHook.cs` file from the `Models` folder.
2. Add the following `using` statements:
   ```
   using System;
   using System.Collections.Generic;
   using System.Linq;
   using System.Text;
   using System.Threading.Tasks;
   ```

3. Change namespace to the following:

    `FishHooksAPI.Models`

4. Add the following properties:

    ```
    public string HookName { get; set; }
    public string BestSpecies { get; set; }
    public string HookDetails { get; set; }
    ```

5. Save the file.
6. Open the `FishHooksViewModel.cs` file from the `ViewModels` folder.
7. Add the following `using` statements:

    ```
    using FishHooksAPI.Models;
    using System;
    using System.Collections.Generic;
    using System.Collections.ObjectModel;
    using System.Linq;
    using System.Text;
    using System.Threading.Tasks;
    ```

8. Change namespace to the following:

    `FishHooksAPI.ViewModels`

9. Add the following property:

    ```
    public ObservableCollection<FishHook> FishHooks
    { get; set; }
    ```

10. Inside the constructor, add the following code:

    ```
    FishHooks = new ObservableCollection<FishHook>();
    FishHooks.Add(new FishHook
    {
        HookName = "Worm Hook",
        BestSpecies = "Largemouth Bass, Smallmouth Bass,
          Speckled Trout, Redfish",
        HookDetails = "The best all-around bass hook. Can be
          used to rig plastics in numerous ways. Usable in
            weeds, rocks, and timber."
    });
    //More object definitions are available in the accompanying
      code packet.
    ```

11. Save the file.
12. Open the `FishHooksPage.cs` file from the `Views` folder.

Working with Xamarin.Forms

13. Add the following `using` statements:

    ```
    using FishHooksAPI.Models;
    using FishHooksAPI.ViewModels;
    using System;
    using System.Collections.Generic;
    using System.Linq;
    using System.Text;
    using System.Threading.Tasks;
    using Xamarin.Forms;
    ```

14. Change namespace to the following:

    ```
    FishHooksAPI.Views
    ```

15. Make the class inherit from `ContentPage` as shown in the following line of code:

    ```
    public class FishHooksPage : ContentPage
    ```

16. Add the following code to the constructor:

    ```
    Title = "Fish Hooks";
    var list = new ListView();
    var viewModel = new FishHooksViewModel();
    list.ItemsSource = viewModel.FishHooks;
    var cell = new DataTemplate(typeof(TextCell));
    cell.SetBinding(TextCell.TextProperty, "HookName");
    list.ItemTemplate = cell;
    list.ItemTapped += (sender, args) =>
    {
    var fishHook = args.Item as FishHook;
    if (fishHook == null)
    {
    return;
    }
    Navigation.PushAsync(new FishHookDetails(fishHook));
    list.SelectedItem = null;
    };
    Content = list;
    ```

17. Save the file. Note that at this time, your application will have errors and cannot be built.

18. Open the `FishHookDetails.cs` file from the `Views` folder.

19. Add the following using statements:

    ```
    using FishHooksAPI.Models;
    using System;
    using System.Collections.Generic;
    using System.Linq;
    using System.Text;
    using System.Threading.Tasks;
    using Xamarin.Forms;
    ```

20. Change namespace to the following:

    ```
    FishHooksAPI.Views
    ```

21. Make the class inherit from ContentPage as shown in the following line of code:

    ```
    public class FishHookDetails : ContentPage
    ```

22. Add the following parameter to the constructor:

    ```
    FishHook fishHook
    ```

23. Add the following code to the constructor:

    ```
    this.Title = fishHook.HookName;
    StringBuilder sb = new StringBuilder();
    sb.Append ("Best used for: ")
       .AppendLine().Append(fishHook.BestSpecies).AppendLine()
         .AppendLine();
    sb.Append ("Hook details: ")
       .AppendLine().Append(fishHook.HookDetails).AppendLine()
         .AppendLine();
    var details = new Label
    {
    Text = sb.ToString()
    };
    Content = new ScrollView
    {
    Padding = 20,
    Content = details
    };
    ```

24. Save the file.

Now, your files and folders are ready, but you still need to tie it all together. To do that, you need to edit the `App.cs` file by performing the following steps:

1. Open the `App.cs` file.
2. Add the following `using` statements:
   ```
   using FishHooksAPI.Views;
   using System;
   using System.Collections.Generic;
   using System.Linq;
   using System.Text;
   using Xamarin.Forms;
   ```
3. Replace the code in `GetMainPage()` with the following code:
   ```
   var fishHooks = new FishHooksPage();
   return new NavigationPage(fishHooks);
   ```
4. Right-click the **iOS** project and choose **Set as startup project**.
5. Run the application in the **Debug** mode.

   Your application's initial screen should look something like the following screenshot:

   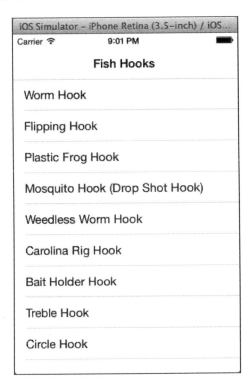

6. If you select one of the hooks, you will see a detail view similar to the following screenshot:

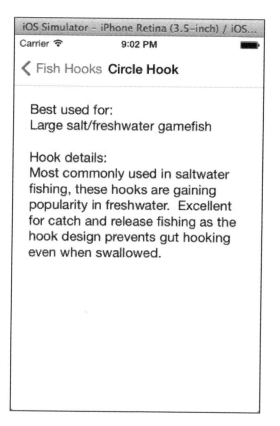

How it works

In this walkthrough, you created your first Xamarin.Forms application that will run on both iOS and Android devices using a single code base. You started by creating folders commonly used in MVVM-based applications.

> The step to create an MVVM-based folder structure is not absolutely necessary, but it's good practice to organize your work. As your applications grow from this simple example into something more complex, these folders will help you to keep your files logically organized. You may also have noticed that your namespaces were created to match this folder structure. Again, this is not a requirement but it is a good practice.

Working with Xamarin.Forms

Next, you added the `FishHook` model. This simple model represents a fishing hook and contains its name, details, and those species of fish the hook is best suited to catch. In order to link your model data to the UI, you need a `ViewModel`. So, you added the `FishHooksViewModel` class. This class contains an `ObservableCollection<T>` object. `ObservableCollection` implements the `INotifyCollectionChanged` and `INotifyPropertyChanged` interfaces, both of which are necessary to support binding under the MVVM model. Inside the `FishHooksViewModel` constructor, you instantiated this collection and began adding `FishHook` objects.

After this, you began to really work with an API to build your app by adding two Pages named `FishHooksPage` and `FishHookDetails`. The `FishHooksPage` Page contains a list of every object in `ViewModel`, while `FishHookDetails` displays the details of each of those models. The `FishHooksPage` class contains two critical components for our discussion. First, you created a new `ListView` object and set the `ItemsSource` property to an instance of `FishHooksViewModel`. Then, the `ListView` object's `ItemTapped` event handler was defined. In this definition, you called `Navigation.PushAsync` by passing in a new instance of the `FishHookDetails` view and the `fishhook` object the user selected.

Then, you created a new `cell` object based on `TextCell.DataTemplate`, and then bound the properties of that cell using the `SetBinding()` method. An instance of this cell will be created to populate the `ListView` object for each object in `FishHooks.ObservableCollection` on the `ViewModel`.

In the `FishHookDetails` file, you set the page title to the `FishHook.HookName` property of the object that is passed into the constructor. Then, you added a `Label` object and set the `Text` property to a custom string based on the details of the `FishHook` object.

Your last code changes occurred in the `App.cs` file, where you replaced the default code inside the `GetMainPage()` method with calls to create a new instance of the `FishHooksPage` object. Next, you created a new `NavigationPage` object and passed in the `FishHooksPage` object as the new root Page.

Finally, you set the iOS project as the startup project. Setting either the iOS or Android project as startup is a necessary step because the main project is not executable. Note that this is the only thing you needed to do with the iOS or Android projects in order to get this application to function on either platform. Although, it is possible (and highly important) to eventually write custom code for each platform, it is not strictly necessary to do so in order to get a fully functioning application up and running.

The XAML design

If you have experience creating applications in WPF, Silverlight, or Windows Store apps, then you may be more comfortable building your applications using the Xamarin.Forms XAML. Unfortunately, there currently isn't a visual XAML designer. So, for the time being we have to create our XAML markups by hand, but that could change in time.

 Note that the Xamarin.Forms XAML is somewhat of a subset to the XAML you may be familiar with, and it also includes new markup tags and attributes created specifically for the Xamarin.Forms framework. I mentioned this to point out that you won't be able to simply import your XAML code files from other solutions and compile them in Xamarin.Forms without significant refactoring.

Let's create the same fishing hooks application as before, but this time create the Pages using XAML. Since the namespaces will change for this project, I will take the time to detail each step again:

1. In Xamarin Studio, create a new solution. Choose the **Blank App (Xamarin.Forms Portable)** project template by navigating to **C# | Mobile Apps**.
2. Name your project FishHooksXAML and click the **OK** button.
3. Add the same three new folders named Models, ViewModels, and Views to the FishHooksAPI project.
4. Right-click the Models folder and choose **New File** under **Add**.
5. Choose the **Empty Class** file type under **General**.
6. Name your file FishHook and click the **OK** button.
7. Right-click the ViewModels folder and choose **New File** under **Add**.
8. Choose the **Empty Class** file type under **General**.
9. Name your file FishHooksViewModel and click the **OK** button.
10. Right-click the Views folder and choose **New File** under **Add**.
11. Choose the **Forms ContentPage Xaml** file type by navigating to **Views | Forms**.
12. Name your file FishHooksPage and click the **OK** button.
13. Right-click the Views folder and choose **New File** under **Add**.
14. Choose the **Forms ContentPage Xaml** file type by navigating to **Views | Forms**.
15. Name your file FishHookDetails and click the **OK** button.

Working with Xamarin.Forms

Your solution should have all of the necessary files and folders at this time. Now let's build the files by performing the following steps:

1. Open the `FishHook.cs` file from the `Models` folder.
2. Add the following using statements:
   ```
   using System;
   using System.Collections.Generic;
   using System.Linq;
   using System.Text;
   using System.Threading.Tasks;
   ```
3. Change namespace to the following:
   ```
   FishHooksXAML.Models
   ```
4. Add the following properties:
   ```
   public string HookName { get; set; }
   public string BestSpecies { get; set; }
   public string HookDetails { get; set; }
   ```
5. Save the file.
6. Open the `FishHooksViewModel.cs` file from the `ViewModels` folder.
7. Add the following using statements:
   ```
   using FishHooksXAML.Models;
   using System;
   using System.Collections.Generic;
   using System.Collections.ObjectModel;
   using System.Linq;
   using System.Text;
   using System.Threading.Tasks;
   ```
8. Change namespace to the following:
   ```
   FishHooksXAML.ViewModels
   ```
9. Add the following property:
   ```
   public ObservableCollection<FishHook> FishHooks
   { get; set; }
   ```
10. Inside the constructor, add the following code:
    ```
    FishHooks = new ObservableCollection<FishHook>();
    FishHooks.Add(new FishHook
    {
        HookName = "Worm Hook",
    ```

```
            BestSpecies = "Largemouth Bass, Smallmouth Bass,
              Speckled Trout, Redfish",
            HookDetails = "The best all-around bass hook. Can be
              used to rig plastics in numerous ways. Usable in
                weeds, rocks, and timber."
    });
    //More object definitions are available in the accompanying
      code packet.
```

11. Save the file.

12. Open the `FishHooksPage.cs` file from the `Views` folder.

13. Add the following using statements to the `FishHooksPage.xaml.cs` file:
    ```
    using FishHooksXAML.Models;
    using FishHooksXAML.ViewModels;
    using System;
    using System.Collections.Generic;
    using Xamarin.Forms;
    ```

14. Change namespace to the following:
    ```
    FishHooksXAML.Views
    ```

15. Make the class inherit from `ContentPage` as shown in the following line of code:
    ```
    public class FishHooksPage : ContentPage
    ```

16. Add the following code to the constructor below the `InitializeComponent()` call:
    ```
    this.BindingContext = new FishHooksViewModel();
    ```

17. Add the `OnItemsSelected()` event handler:
    ```
    public void OnItemSelected(object sender, ItemTappedEventArgs
    args)
    {
        var fishHook = args.Item as FishHook;
        if (fishHook == null)
        {
            return;
        }
        Navigation.PushAsync(new FishHookDetails(fishHook));
        list.SelectedItem = null;
    }
    ```

18. Save the file. Note that at this time, your application will have errors and cannot be built.

Working with Xamarin.Forms

19. If the `FishHooksPage.xaml` file is not open, open it now.
20. Replace the existing `ContentPage` with the following code:

    ```
    <ContentPage
        xmlns="http://xamarin.com/schemas/2014/forms"
        xmlns:x="http://schemas.microsoft.com/winfx/2009/xaml"
        x:Class="FishHooksXAML.Views.FishHooksPage"
        xmlns:local="clr-
            namespace:FishHooksXAML.Views;assembly=FishHooksXAML"
        Title="Fish Hooks">
    ```

21. Replace the contents of the `ContentPage` tag with the following code:

    ```
    <ListView x:Name="list" ItemsSource="{Binding FishHooks}"
      ItemTapped="OnItemSelected">
        <ListView.ItemTemplate>
           <DataTemplate>
              <TextCell Text="{Binding HookName}">
           </TextCell>
           </DataTemplate>
        </ListView.ItemTemplate>
     </ListView>
    ```

22. Save the file. Note that at this time, your application will have errors and cannot be built.
23. Open the `FishHookDetails.cs` file from the `Views` folder.
24. Add the following using statements to the `FishHookDetails.xaml.cs` file:

    ```
    using FishHooksAPI.Models;
    using System;
    using System.Collections.Generic;
    using Xamarin.Forms;
    ```

25. Change namespace to the following:

    ```
    FishHooksXAML.Views
    ```

26. Make the class inherit from `ContentPage` as shown in the following code:

    ```
    public class FishHookDetails : ContentPage
    ```

27. Add the following parameter to the constructor:

    ```
    public FishHookDetails(FishHook fishHook)
    ```

28. Add the following code to the constructor below the `InitializeComponent()` call:

    ```
    this.BindingContext = fishHook;
    ```

29. Save the file.
30. If the `FishHookDetails.xaml` file is not open, open it now.
31. Replace the existing `ContentPage` node with the following code:
    ```
    <ContentPage
        xmlns="http://xamarin.com/schemas/2014/forms"
        xmlns:x="http://schemas.microsoft.com/winfx/2009/xaml"
        x:Class="FishHooksXAML.Views.FishHookDetails"
        xmlns:local="clr-
          namespace:FishHooksXAML.Views;assembly=FishHooksXAML"
        Title="{Binding HookName}">
    ```
32. Replace the contents of the `ContentPage` tag with the following code:
    ```
    <ScrollView Padding="20">
        <StackLayout VerticalOptions="FillAndExpand"
           Spacing="10">
         <Label Text="Best used for:" />
         <Label Text="{Binding BestSpecies}" />
           <Label Text="Hook details:" />
           <Label Text="{Binding HookDetails}" />
        </StackLayout>
      </ScrollView>
    ```

Now your solution has everything in place. But again, you need to tie it all together using the `App.cs` file by performing the following steps:

1. Open the `App.cs` file.
2. Add the following `using` statements:
    ```
    using FishHooksXAML.Views;
    using System;
    using System.Collections.Generic;
    using System.Linq;
    using System.Text;
    using Xamarin.Forms;
    ```
3. Replace the code in `GetMainPage()` with the following code:
    ```
    var fishHooks = new FishHooksPage();
    return new NavigationPage(fishHooks);
    ```
4. Now, you can run your application on an Android platform. Right-click the **Android** project and choose **Set as startup project**.

5. Run the application in the **Debug** mode.

   Your application's initial screen should look something like the following screenshot:

6. If you select one of the hooks, you will see a detail view similar to the following screenshot:

   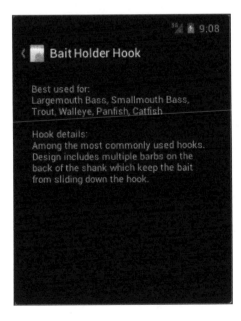

How it works

The folder structure and the `FishHook` and `FishHooksViewModel` classes you created for this example are identical to those that you created when building the application using the API, except that you used different namespaces. In fact, even the code in the `App.cs` file is identical in both approaches because the compiler can tell the difference between the API-based files and XAML files without any extra development effort on your part. This is an excellent feature because it means you can develop your applications with both the API and XAML files side by side, without worrying about managing divergent code branches to handle each.

The only difference in this application is the use of XAML instead of the API, so we will focus on the two `ContentPage` files you added. First, you added `FishHooksPage.xaml` and its code-behind file `FishHooksPage.xaml.cs`. There are several important items to review in these two files. In the code-behind file's constructor, you set the `BindingContext` property to an instance of the `FishHooksViewModel` class. The `BindingContext` property tells the compiler where to find the properties referenced by bindings in the XAML file. Next, you added the event handler for `OnItemSelected()`. This event handler intercepts a user tap event on the cells in your `ListView` object, and in turn uses the `Navigation` object to asynchronously push a new instance of the `FishHookDetails` Page.

Next, in the XAML file, you might have noticed that the `x:Class` attribute did not include the correct namespace. This is to be expected because you changed the namespace in the code-behind file manually after you created the file. Just remember that whenever you change the namespace, you need to also update the `x:Class` attribute in the XAML file; otherwise, you will get build errors. Also, the `xmlns:local` attribute was originally missing from the `ContentPage` tag altogether. This attribute is crucial for properly linking the code-behind file to the XAML, and you must take care when creating your Pages to ensure that it is properly formatted. In fact, the most common (and annoying) errors I have encountered when working with XAML and code-behind files were due to this attribute being improperly formatted.

Finally, you nested a `ListView` object control inside the `ContentPage` tag. This `ListView` control contains a `TextCell` control for each object in the `FishHooksViewModel.FishHooks` collection. The `TextCell.Text` property contains the object's `HookName` property via the `{Binding HookName}` data binding.

The second content file you added was `FishHookDetails.xaml` and its code-behind file `FishHookDetails.xaml.cs`. In the code-behind file's constructor, you set the `BindingContext` property to the `FishHook` object that was passed in. In the XAML file, you edited the `ContentPage` tag again, updating the `x:Class` attribute and adding the `xmlns:local` attribute. Finally, you nested a `StackLayout` panel inside the `ContentPage` control. Inside this panel, you stacked four labels to display information on each hook. Details of each hook are bound to the labels' `Text` properties using the same `{Binding BestSpecies}` and `{Binding HookDetails}` data bindings.

> For more information on Xamarin.Forms and example applications built using the framework, check out Xamarin's documentation at http://developer.xamarin.com/guides/cross-platform/xamarin-forms/.

Summary

In this chapter, we briefly reviewed the Xamarin.Forms framework introduced by Xamarin 3. We looked at the requirements for using the framework in terms of licensing subscriptions, as well as the components and controls provided by the framework. Finally, you created two simple cross-platform applications using the built-in UI design APIs as well as the XAML design approaches.

In the next chapter, we will take a detailed look at application states and the lifecycles for iOS and Android applications.

Application Lifecycle

In this chapter, we will cover the following topics:

- The iOS application lifecycle
- UIViewController lifecycle methods
- The Android application lifecycle
- Activity lifecycle methods
- Background state

In this chapter, we're going to spend some time examining applications' states, lifecycles, and multitasking on mobile devices. Although this may seem like a detour from learning about the development environment, Xamarin Studio developers must understand these concepts to successfully build cross-platform apps. This chapter is not intended to introduce every aspect of lifecycles and multitasking in a mobile environment. It is intended to introduce those core concepts that are, in my experience, most critical and potentially confusing to a .NET developer being introduced to iOS and Android development for the first time. Using this knowledge as a foundation, we'll then be able to move on to testing and deployment in *Chapter 7, Testing and Debugging*, and *Chapter 8, Deployment*, respectively.

By the end of this chapter, you should be familiar with the application states, the View/Activity lifecycles for iOS and Android apps, as well as the events and corresponding methods you need to implement to handle transitions. You should also be familiar with the difference between foreground and background states and how to prepare your applications to present a seamless flow between the two.

The iOS application lifecycle

To begin, let's first have a look at the following iOS application lifecycle flowchart:

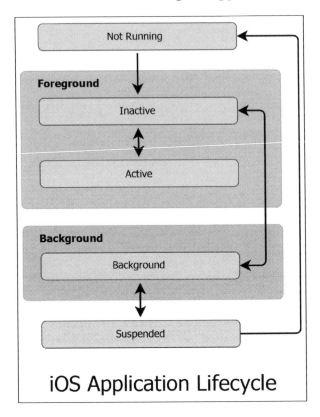

The application lifecycle includes all of the activity in an app from the time it is deployed until the time it has been removed from a device. Each platform describes the lifecycle in varying terms. In the case of an iOS device, the lifecycle is a collection of application states and methods that must be observed while transitioning between those states. Using the previous image as a reference, iOS apps will always exist in one of the following five states:

- **Not running**: This means your app has either not been launched, or it has been terminated by the system for some reason. If your app is currently not running, it can be transitioned into the inactive state when it's launched.
- **Inactive**: This occurs while the app is in the foreground but does not receive event updates. It also occurs when the device screen automatically turns off to conserve power. This state is usually short-lived, and typically occurs during the transitions between other states. Apps that are currently inactive can transition into either the active or background state.

- **Active (Running)**: This is the normal operating mode for your iOS applications. While in the active mode, your app is running in the foreground and receiving events from the system. Active apps can only transition into an inactive state.
- **Background**: This state encompasses the time your app is not active, but still executes code. Most apps enter this state briefly prior to being suspended, although an app may request extra execution time to run additional processes while in this state. It is also possible to launch an app directly into this state intentionally to avoid entering the inactive state. An app in the background can transition into either the inactive or suspended state. For more information on background state, see the *The background state* section later in this chapter.

> Please note that apps can only enter the background state on devices that support multitasking, or those that run iOS 4.0 or later.

- **Suspended**: Apps in this state are in the background but they don't execute code or receive events. An app can be suspended while in the background if it has no tasks to run or if those tasks have been completed. The system can move an app into this state at any time without notifying the app that it is doing so. During a low memory situation, the system might, without notice, purge apps from the memory that are in this state. This typically only occurs when an app running in the foreground needs additional system resources. Suspended apps can transition into the background or be terminated by the system as required.

The AppDelegate class

Whenever your application transitions from one state to another, there is usually an associated event accompanying that transition. In order to respond to these events, you must implement the appropriate methods in your `AppDelegate` class. The `AppDelegate` object provides a centralized location to coordinate behaviors throughout your application, and is instantiated by the `Main` class when your app first launches. You can think of it as a sort of master controller, responsible for listening to any event notifications coming from the operating system. It is extremely important, and in some cases required, to respond to these events in order to maintain the stability of your app and any user data.

- `OnActivated()`: This function is called both when the app is launched and whenever it returns to the foreground. This method gives your app the first opportunity to execute code at launch time. Additionally, this method is generally the place where you should ensure that all resources and state information required for foreground execution are available and configured.

Application Lifecycle

- `WillEnterForeground()`: This function is called immediately after an app returns from a background state. The `OnActivated()` function will be called immediately after this call is completed.
- `WillFinishLaunching()`: This function is called when a launch has been initiated, but the state restoration hasn't been completed.
- `FinishedLaunching()`: This function is invoked after the application has launched and loaded, and the UI is ready to run. This is where you must configure the main top-level window. This top-level window requires a root `UIViewController` object, which must also be configured here.

> Do not try to perform too much work using this method! Once this method is called, you only have 17 seconds to complete the tasks contained therein. If your code execution lingers here for more than 17 seconds, the operating system will terminate your application without any notification.

- `OnResignActivation()`: This function is called whenever the app is interrupted by a system event, such as an incoming phone call or text message. It is also called whenever the app is about to be suspended or moved into the background state. If you have created any expensive resources, you will need to release them here to ensure that the application is in a consistent and restorable state. If you are running an OpenGL application, you should use this method to pause the game.
- `DidEnterBackground()`: This function is called whenever the app enters the background state. The system only gives you 5 seconds to complete this method, or your app will be terminated without notification. You should use these 5 seconds wisely to save user data, tasks, and the application state, and remove any sensitive information from the view. If your app doesn't support background execution, `DidEnterBackground()` will not be called; instead, `WillTerminate()` will be called.
- `WillTerminate()`: This function is called when the app is about to be terminated. On rare occasions, the system will terminate the app due to memory constraints. More commonly, though, termination is directed by the user. If you have any data that needs to be saved, this method is your last chance to do so.

[146]

UIViewController lifecycle methods

The following is a flowchart depicting a `UIViewController` lifecycle:

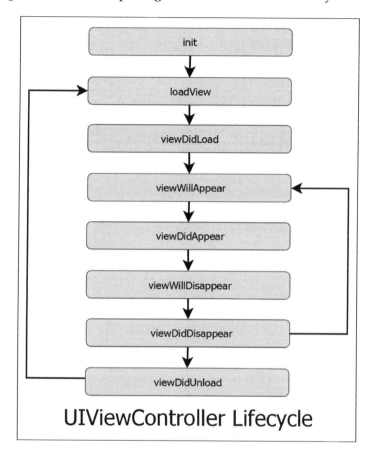

UIViewController Lifecycle

The `UIViewController` class is the base class responsible for managing the communication between model and view classes in an iOS. A View's lifecycle is defined by several methods that can be overridden in any class that inherits from `UIViewController`. While you are loading a view into the display, these events will fire in the order they are listed here:

- `ViewDidLoad()`: This is arguably the most important event in any UIView's lifecycle. This method is called when the view and its entire display hierarchy have been loaded into memory, whether the view was created programmatically or loaded from a XIB file. This method is a good place to wire up event handlers and create any additional views that were not created programmatically or in the XIB file. Also, this is where you should do any configuration work that could not be done in the XIB file.

- `ViewWillAppear()`: This event is called prior to the view being added to the display hierarchy. If you override this method, you must always call `base.ViewWillAppear()`. Any tasks that you wouldn't want to occur when the view isn't on the screen should be handled here. For example, if your view needs to subscribe to any notifications, you probably don't want to do that unless the view is actually going to be visible.
- `ViewDidAppear()`: This event is called once the view is added to the display hierarchy. If you override this method, you must always call `base.ViewDidAppear()`.

Likewise, while you are unloading a view from the display, you should observe these methods:

- `ViewWillDisappear()`: This method is called prior to removing the view from the display hierarchy. If you override this method, you must always call `base.ViewWillDisappear()`. It's a good idea to undo anything that you implemented in `ViewWillAppear()` or `ViewDidAppear()`.
- `ViewDidDisappear()`: This method is called after the view is removed from the display hierarchy.

Another method that you should consider overriding is `DidReceieveMemoryWarning()`. This is a good place to clear any caches or unload large view hierarchies that can be reconstructed later. This method can also be called if the view has already disappeared from the screen, which would normally occur if you have left large objects in memory and the system needs to dispose them to make room for other processes. If you override this method, you must always call `base.DidReceiveMemoryWarning()`.

Examining iOS lifecycles

In this exercise, we will build a single-view application so that we can examine the lifecycles of an iOS application and a simple `UIViewController`:

1. Create a new iPhone single-view application and name it `iOSLifecycles`.
2. Your solution should open the `AppDelegate` class. In this class, you will see four empty methods. Inside each of those methods, insert a line of code similar to the following, replacing `OnResignActivation()` with the name of the method you are modifying:

   `Console.WriteLine("OnResignActiviation()");`

3. Next, add the following class-level property to the `AppDelegate` class:

   `iOSLifecyclesViewController viewController;`

4. Add the following two methods to the `AppDelegate` class:

```
public override void OnActivated(UIApplication application)
{
   Console.WriteLine("OnActivated()");
}

public override bool FinishedLaunching(UIApplication app,
   NSDictionary options)
{
   Window = new UIWindow (UIScreen.MainScreen.Bounds);
   viewController = new iOSLifecyclesViewController();
   Window.RootViewController = viewController;
   Window.MakeKeyAndVisible ();
   Console.WriteLine("App has finished launching.");
   return true;
}
```

5. Open the `iOSLifeCyclesViewController` class. You will see empty methods for `ViewWillAppear()`, `ViewDidAppear()`, `ViewWillDisappear()`, and `ViewDidDisappear()`. Inside each of the four methods, insert a line of code similar to the following, replacing `ViewWillAppear()` with the name of the method you are modifying:

```
Console.WriteLine("ViewWillAppear()");
```

6. Finally, add a default constructor to `iOSLifeCyclesViewController`:

```
public iOSLifecyclesViewController()
{
}
```

Examining the application lifecycle

Run the app and examine the output of the application in the **Application Output** tab. Since you began with an **iOS Single-View Application** project template, but you haven't added anything yet to the view, your app will load a black screen (don't panic!), while the **Application Output** window will log events as they occur. Your output will look similar to the following:

```
ViewDidLoad()
ViewWillAppear()
App has finished launching.
OnActivated()
ViewDidAppear()
```

At this stage, your app is in the active state. If you hit the **Home** button on your device, your app will be moved into the background state. Your output window should now have the following additional entries:

```
OnResignActivation()
DidEnterBackground()
```

If your app has any background code to run, it will remain in the background state until those tasks are completed. Since you have not added any code to be run in the background, your app will be moved immediately to the suspended state.

The Android application lifecycle

Most programming paradigms involve a `main()` method that activates an app and launches it into the memory. In the case of Android, however, the system creates and manages an application object. This object initiates code in an Activity instance by invoking specific callback methods that correspond to specific stages of the Activity's lifecycle. This means that the lifecycle of the application is directly linked to the lifecycle of the foreground Activity.

Understanding application lifecycle

The system creates an application object for each app that's running. This object remains in the memory for the life of the application process, and will always exist in one of the following five possible process statuses at any given time. These statuses are each assigned a priority, which is used exclusively by the system when it needs to determine which processes can be terminated to recover resources:

- **Foreground**: Any process that has an Activity in the foreground, which is the Activity on top of the screen the user is currently interacting with, receives the highest priority. This process will only be terminated by the operating system as a last resort if it uses more resources than those available on the device.

- **Visible**: Processes with a **Visible** Activity, which is an Activity that is visible to the user but not in the foreground, is next on the priority list. This process will not be terminated unless it is absolutely necessary to keep the foreground process running. Activities can be transitioned into the **Visible** state when they become partially obscured by another Activity.

- **Service**: Occasionally, an Activity will need to perform a long-running operation, which is not directly linked to the Activity itself. An example might be an application that uploads photos to a social networking site, but allows the user to leave the application while displaying progress notifications in the status bar. To achieve this, your Activity should create a Service. The system will prioritize a service process above other invisible processes until the task is completed, independent of whether the Activity is still running or not.

- **Background**: Below the Service process is the Background process. A background process contains an Activity, which has been paused and is not visible to the user. This process is not considered critical, so the system can safely terminate the thread as needed to recover system resources. As we will see later in this chapter, before an app becomes a Background process, the state of the application should be saved using the `OnSavedInstanceState(Bundle)` method. Then, when the user opens the application again, the main Activity's `OnCreate(Bundle)` method can restore the app to its previous state. This functionality can provide the appearance of a seamless transition from Active to Background to Active again, even though the app may have been terminated at some point along the way.

- **Empty**: Finally, an **Empty** process has no Activities or other application components (such as a Service or BroadcastReceiver object). As resources begin to become scarce, the operating system will view these apps as the low hanging fruit. They will be terminated very quickly to recover resources needed by application objects with higher priorities. This is why critical background tasks that need to occur outside of an Activity must be performed within the context of a Service or BroadcastReceiver.

Activities in Android are managed by the Activity stack. Whenever a new Activity is created, it is pushed onto the stack and becomes the foreground Activity. The previous Activity will remain below the current Activity until the foreground Activity is popped. Activities have four states:

- Activities running in the foreground that the user is interacting with are in the active or running state. These Activities are on top of the Activity stack.

- Activities that have lost focus but are still visible are in a paused state. Activities are transitioned to the paused state when a new transparent Activity, or an Activity that isn't full sized, is pushed onto the stack above your Activity. A paused Activity is still completely functional in terms of internal processes, although a user cannot interact directly with it. It will maintain all of its state and member information and will remain attached to the window manager. However, a paused Activity can be terminated by the system if the active Activity needs additional resources.

- When an Activity is completely covered by another, it transitions into the stopped or background state. It will continue to maintain all state and member information, but is no longer visible to the user. Its window will be hidden and it will very likely be terminated by the system when additional resources are required for an active Activity.
- Whenever an Activity is in the paused or stopped states, the system can terminate its process by either asking the process to finish, or by just killing it outright. When this occurs, the Activity is transitioned to the killed state. If the app opens an Activity that is in a killed state, the Activity must be completely restarted and restored to its previous state.

Activity lifecycle methods

The following is a flowchart of an Android Activity lifecycle:

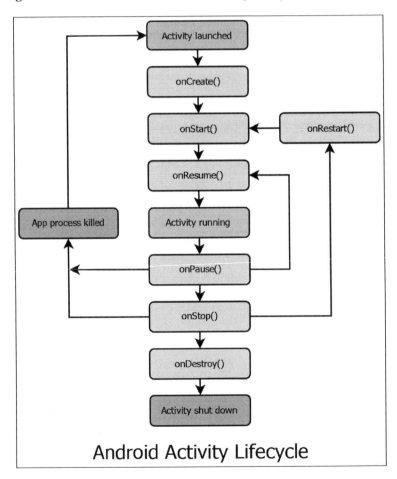

As an Android developer using Xamarin Studio, it is critical to have a firm understanding of the Activity lifecycle and its associated methods. Although the entire lifecycle of an Activity includes many methods, you will only work with a few key items on a regular basis:

- OnCreate(): This method is called when an Activity is created. This is where you must set all of your static content, including the creation of views, binding data to lists, initializing variables, and so on. This method also provides you with a data object called Bundle. The Bundle is a dictionary object containing the Activity's previously frozen state, if one exists. When an Activity is operating in this method, the system cannot terminate it. This method is always followed immediately by the OnStart() method.

- OnStart(): This method is fired as the Activity becomes visible to the user. When an Activity is operating in this state, it cannot be terminated by the system. Your Activity should override this method if you have logic that needs to be implemented precisely before the Activity becomes visible. This method is followed by either the OnResume() method if the Activity moves into the foreground, or the OnStop() method if the Activity is hidden.

- OnRestart(): This method is similar to the OnStart() method, except it only occurs when the Activity was previously running but has been terminated by the system. There are no hard rules for what type of code should be implemented in the OnRestart() method. This is because OnStart() is always called, whether the Activity is being created or recreated. Therefore, unless you have logic that is specific to a restart scenario, you should implement all of your startup logic in the OnStart() method to avoid code duplication. When an Activity is operating in this method, the system cannot terminate it, and it is always immediately followed by the onStart() method.

- OnResume(): This method is called when the Activity is on top of the Activity stack and about to begin interacting with the user. Activities should use this method for tasks such as listening for GPS updates, displaying alerts or dialogs, wiring up external event handlers, and so on. Any actions implemented in the OnPause() method must be undone in the OnResume() method. When an Activity is operating in this state, it cannot be terminated by the system. This method is always followed by the OnPause() method.

- `OnPause()`: This method is called as the Activity is placed in the background or becomes obscured. Typically, you will use this method to commit unsaved changes to persistent data stores, stop CPU intensive processes, unregister external events, or ramp down frame rates. Additionally, any alerts or dialogs that were created by your Activity must be destroyed here using the `Dismiss()` method. Be aware that the code in this method must be executed quickly, because the next Activity will not resume until this call returns. In Android versions prior to Level 14 (Honeycomb), the system can terminate Activities operating in this method. From Level 14 and above, however, the system cannot terminate the Activity until it has returned from the `OnStop()` method. The `OnPause()` method is followed by either `OnResume()` if the Activity returns to the front, or `OnStop()` if it becomes invisible.

- `OnStop()`: This method is called only after the Activity is not visible to the user due to another Activity covering it. There is a chance that `OnStop()` will not be called in a resource-starved situation, so you should not rely on it to prepare an Activity for destruction. This method is followed by either `OnRestart()` when the Activity is returning to interact with the user, or `OnDestroy()` if the Activity is being terminated.

- `OnDestroy()`: This is the last call you will receive, which occurs just before your Activity is destroyed. Be aware there is no guarantee this method will be called, so you should not depend on it to perform any critical functions. The system can terminate an Activity running in this method. No other methods follow `OnDestroy()`.

Conceptually, these methods can be grouped into three loops of behavior. The entire lifetime of an Activity takes place between the first call to `OnCreate()` and the last call to `OnDestroy()`. An Activity will set up all the global state information in `OnCreate()`, and release all resources in `OnDestroy()`. For example, if an Activity has a thread running in a background process for the purpose of downloading data from a network location, the Activity can create the thread in the `OnCreate()` method and then stop the thread in `OnDestroy()`.

The visible lifetime of an Activity occurs between the call to `OnStart()` and a matching call to `OnStop()`. This loop represents the time for which a user can see the Activity on the screen, even though the Activity may not be in the foreground where the user is interacting with it. These two methods can be called multiple times as the Activity transitions between visible and hidden. Between these methods, you can maintain the resources required to display the Activity to the user. For example, you can register a `BroadcastReceiver` in `OnStart()` to listen to notifications affecting the UI, and unregister it in `OnStop()` when the Activity is no longer visible.

Finally, the foreground lifetime of an Activity occurs between a call to `OnStart()` or `OnResume()` and a matching call to `OnPause()`. These methods encompass the time that the Activity is on top of the Activity stack. As a general rule, these methods should be kept lean, because an Activity will transition between the resumed and paused states frequently through the course of its lifecycle.

Configuration changes

To add another complication, an Android Activity will be destroyed and recreated in response to a special event known as a configuration change. Configuration changes happen much more frequently than their name implies. Device rotation, showing or hiding the keyboard, or even placing the device in a dock are some of the more common physical events that can trigger a rapid configuration change. To maintain a seamless user experience, it is extremely important that the state of your Activities be stored and restored quickly in response to these events. This saved state of an Activity is called an instance state.

Primitive values in an instance state can be stored using a dictionary object called the Bundle, and your Activity has two methods to store and retrieve these values. First, `OnSaveStateInstance()` is called by the system while the Activity is being destroyed, and this is where you will place the logic to store your data using key/value pairs in the Bundle. This method is complimented by `OnRestoreInstance()`, which is called once the `OnCreate()` method is finished. Once initialization is complete, this method allows you to rehydrate your stored Activity state from the values stored in the Bundle.

In scenarios where larger, more complex data structures are being stored, or where it is expensive in terms of resources to retrieve data multiple times, you can override the `OnRetainNonConfigurationInstance()` method. The objects returned by this method are retained by memory, eliminating the need for repeated round trips to the data source, whether that source is a local data cache or a remote web service.

Examining application states

In this exercise, we will build a basic Android application so that we can examine the lifecycles of an Android Activity:

1. Create a new Android Ice Cream Sandwich Application and name it `ActivityLifecycle`.

2. Your solution should open in the `MainActivity.cs` class, which contains an override for `OnCreate(bundle)`. Inside this method, insert a line of code similar to the following:

   ```
   Console.WriteLine("OnCreate()");
   ```

3. Next, add the following methods:
   ```
   protected override void OnStart()
   {
       Console.WriteLine("OnStart()");
       base.OnStart();
   }
   protected override void OnResume()
   {
       Console.WriteLine("OnResume()");
       base.OnResume();
   }
   protected override void OnPause()
   {
       Console.WriteLine("OnPause()");
       base.OnPause();
   }
   protected override void OnStop()
   {
       Console.WriteLine("OnStop()");
       base.OnStop();
   }
   protected override void OnDestroy ()
   {
       base.OnDestroy();
       Console.WriteLine("OnDestroy()");
   }
   ```
4. Run your application. When prompted, be sure to start and select a device running API Level 15 or above.

Examining the Activity lifecycle

Run the app and examine the output of the application in the **Application Output** tab. Since you began with a basic **Android Ice Cream Sandwich** project template, your app will launch with a button and label in the display, but you can ignore these for now. The **Application Output** window will log application and Activity level events as they occur. At this stage, your output will look similar to the following:

```
OnCreate()
OnStart()
OnResume()
```

If you hit the **Home** button on your device, you will see the methods that fire while the app is moving into the background state. These two entries should have been added to your output window:

```
OnPause()
OnStop()
```

Next, reopen the application and click on the **Recent Applications** button. Your app will move to the background this time because it has become partially obscured by the Recent Applications Activity. Reopening the app and clicking on the **Recent Applications** button should add the following four entries:

```
OnStart()
OnResume()
OnPause()
OnStop()
```

Finally, open the app one last time and hit the **Back** button. This will dismiss the app, adding the following entries:

```
OnStart()
OnResume()
OnPause()
OnStop()
OnDestroy()
```

The patterns demonstrated in your app are predictable and repeatable in any Android application. The only exception to this is that in low-memory scenarios when the system needs to destroy the Activity quickly, OnStop() might not be called.

The background state

Multitasking on a mobile device is profoundly different from that of a desktop machine. Applications on desktop machines have deep system resources to draw from in terms of memory, processor speed, power, and even screen space. Most modern desktops can run multiple applications concurrently, allowing each application to operate efficiently and remain responsive to user interaction. The limited resources on a mobile device, however, require the system to closely monitor how applications are functioning, policing their use of system assets in a much stricter manner. Therefore, if an application is not at the foreground of the device, the system will place it in the background state. On iOS devices, this transition is called backgrounding, while on Android devices it is referred to as background processing. For the remainder of this discussion, we will use the terms backgrounded and backgrounding generically to describe the behavior on both platforms.

When an app is in the background, it is placed in a state where it can continue to perform various processes, but it can also be terminated by the system as needed. Backgrounding can be initiated by several sources. First, the app itself can request to be in the background. For example, in order to protect sensitive data an app can be designed to timeout following a prescribed period of user inactivity. Or maybe the app is simply designed to launch a service that resides in the background until a notification is received. An app can also be backgrounded at the request of a user, such as when the user hits the Home or Sleep buttons on an iOS device. Finally, the app can be backgrounded in the direction of the system when it is interrupted by a higher priority process, such as an incoming phone call or text message.

A detailed discussion on the breadth of backgrounding is a book of its own—a thick book. However, there are several generic principles and concerns common to all mobile devices that should be adhered to. In response to a transition into the background, you must at a minimum ensure that your app addresses the following concerns:

- Saves user data and app state information. If your app is quietly terminated while in the background, all unsaved changes to user data should be written to disk prior to entering the background.
- It should free up as much memory as practical. The system will try to maintain as many of the apps currently running in the memory as possible. However, when the memory begins to run low, backgrounded apps that have the largest memory footprint are typically the first to be terminated.
- It should stop any running timers or other periodic tasks.
- It should stop any queries running against the metadata on your local data store.
- It does not initiate any new tasks.
- If your app is playing a video, playback should be paused.
- If you app is a game, it should transition into a paused state.
- If your app uses OpenGL, it should throttle down ES frame rates.
- Further, any dispatch queues or operational queues running noncritical code paths should be suspended. An exception to this rule would involve apps that have processes designed to operate in the background, such as a social media tool uploading photos to a user's account for example.

Summary

In this chapter, we studied application lifecycles and states for both iOS and Android platforms. For iOS platforms, we examined how the `AppDelegate` class can be used to respond to changes in the application state. Also, we looked at the methods associated with state changes in the `UIViewController` class. For Android platforms, we examined how an application's lifecycle is linked to that of its Activities. We looked at the methods that can be used to respond to changes in an Activity's state, and how to respond to a rapid configuration change event. Finally, we examined backgrounding from a generic point of view including the most important concerns that must be addressed for an app that is transitioning into a background state.

In *Chapter 7, Testing and Debugging*, we're going to discuss the tools available to test your applications including unit test projects, debugging tools, simulators and emulators, crash logs, TestFlight, and platform-specific suites of tools.

7
Testing and Debugging

In this chapter, we will cover the following topics:

- The Xamarin debugger
- Unit tests
- Simulators
- Device testing
- TestFlight
- Instruments
- Device Monitor
- Logs
- Other testing considerations

Unless you plan on independently releasing your apps outside an App Store, your work needs to pass a stringent set of tests and approval processes. Companies such as Apple are more concerned about protecting their business reputations than helping you unleash the next big thing in mobile development on an unsuspecting world. In a nutshell, they're not going to knowingly allow bad code to be published on their sites.

Therefore, in this chapter we're going to look at testing and debugging tools that will help you certify that your app is bulletproof and ready. Some of these tools come packaged with Xamarin 3, such as the built-in debugger and **Unit Test** project templates. Others come with the iOS or Android platform tools that you installed, such as **Instruments** and **Device Monitor**. Others are available from third-party vendors such as TestFlight and TestCloud. Methodologies such as the need to test on physical devices and to do so under variable environmental conditions will also be discussed. Although we won't be able to dig into each of these tools in detail, knowing that they exist and what they are capable of is important enough to justify their inclusion in this chapter.

The Xamarin debugger

Debugging is the systematic process of locating and eliminating bugs in a piece of software with the goal of making the software operate as intended. Debugging is (typically) performed with the help of tools designed for this purpose, which are collectively known as debuggers. While testing your applications in Xamarin, you have two options for debugging. You can choose the debugging tools that come bundled with Xamarin Studio, or you can use the **GNU Debugger (GDB)**.

The Xamarin debugger is a type of soft debugger. Soft debuggers take the compiled code and use it along with the IDE to allow you to debug the application. Although this provides a decent debugging experience, soft debuggers have limitations—they need to actually run the code in order to function. Also, soft debuggers suffer from flaws known as reentrance problems that can cause all sorts of application instability. To compensate for this shortcoming, they are limited by design in the scope that they are permitted to operate in. For example, you typically can't attach to an already running process and you can never debug a core dump. Keeping these shortcomings aside, soft debuggers excel at debugging managed memory code.

GDB, on the other hand, is a type of hard debugger. Hard debugging actually controls the code without the code's knowledge or cooperation. These debuggers can attach themselves to an already running process and they can also debug a core dump. Plus, they are impervious to reentrance issues. As a general rule, you should use the Xamarin tools to debug C# and any other managed memory language code in your application, but use the GDB to debug C, C++, or Objective-C libraries that are linked to your solution.

The debugger tool in Xamarin Studio works in the same way as it would work in any other modern IDE. You set breakpoints by clicking on the gutter of the code window or by adding them through the **Breakpoint** tab. These breakpoints can have conditions attached to them, or they can be left to halt execution every time that line of code is hit. You have the ability to enable and disable the breakpoints, or delete them altogether by clicking them a second time. For more information on setting and modifying breakpoints, please check out the *Information pads* section in *Chapter 2, Learning and Customizing the XS Environment*.

In order to use the debugger, you must select the **Debug** configuration for your platform from the drop-down menu in the IDE toolbar. Then, run your application by either selecting the **Start Debugging** menu option under **Run**, or by simply clicking the **Start** button.

Unit tests

Although most .NET developers are probably familiar with the concept of unit testing, it's worth reviewing briefly here. Generally speaking, unit tests are programs designed to figuratively break apart your application into independent blocks, or units, based on specific functions, and then test those blocks to ensure they function as intended. To put it another way, unit tests allow us to take any function in our application and, given a specific set of inputs, test to ensure that the function is returning the correct values or failing gracefully.

For more information about unit testing, please visit http://www.extremeprogramming.org/rules/unittests.html.

Including unit tests in your solutions offers several advantages. Since unit tests work on small, manageable chunks of code, they naturally train a developer to create methods that are less complex and more focused on a single task. Also, as unit tests exist outside the normal process flow of the application, it's possible to package them in a separate project that can be run at will, without actually running the application itself. This package can even be integrated with a build process to support **continuous integration (CI)**.

For more information about CI, please visit http://www.extremeprogramming.org/rules/integrateoften.html.

Over time, as you create more and more tests, you could have an entire suite of tests that cover large portions of your code that can be executed on demand. This is valuable because it allows you to quickly confirm whether or not changes in your code will break the build, without actually rebuilding the entire solution or performing regression testing. Also, you can run these tests before the code is actually committed to source control. This helps developers to discover errors in our algorithms and logic, long before the code reaches QA or, even worse, the customer. Obviously, all of these advantages come at the cost of additional upfront development effort. Most experienced developers will agree, though, that increased confidence in the code's stability and reduced long-term maintenance more than outweighs the initial investment.

Testing and Debugging

Touch.Unit and Andr.Unit

Xamarin provides two unit test frameworks for you to work with. For iOS development, there is the Touch.Unit framework, based on a modified version of NUnitLite coupled with an iOS test runner. For Android development, there is the Andr.Unit framework. Unfortunately, these two packages are not portable from one platform to another, so you must create separate unit test projects for each platform.

Creating a unit test project

To begin, you need to create your unit test project. To create the project, follow these steps:

1. Navigate to **iOS | iPhone** and create a new **Empty Project** solution.
2. Name this project UnitTestsLibrary.
3. Change the name of the solution to UnitTestsSolution and click the **OK** button.
4. Right-click the solution and add a new project.
5. From the **new object** dialog, open the **iOS** group.
6. Select the **iOS Unit Tests Project** template.
7. Name the project UnitTests and click the **OK** button.
8. Right-click the UnitTestsLibrary project and add a new file.
9. From the **General** group, add a new **Empty Class** to the project.
10. Name the file MethodsForTesting.
11. From the same project, delete the MyClass.cs file.
12. In the UnitTests project, right-click on the **References** folder and choose **Edit References**.
13. In the **Projects** tab, check the UnitTestsLibrary project and click the **OK** button.
14. From the UnitTestLibrary project, open the MethodsForTesting.cs file and add the following code below the constructor:

    ```
    public int AddValues(int x, int y)
    {
      return x + y;
    }

    public int SubtractValues(int x, int y)
    {
    ```

[164]

```
        return x - y;
    }

    public int MultiplyValues(int x, int y)
    {
        return x * y;
    }

    public int DivideValues(int x, int y)
    {
        if (y == 0)
        {
            return 0;
        }
        return x / y;
    }
```

15. From the UnitTest project, open the Tests.cs file and add the following using statement:

    ```
    using UnitTestsLibrary;
    ```

16. Next, add the following code below the existing tests:

    ```
    [Test]
    public void AddValuesTest()
    {
        int x = 9;
        int y = 10;

        MethodsForTesting methods = new MethodsForTesting ();
        int testValue = methods.addValues (x, y);

        Assert.True (testValue == 19);
    }

    [Test]
    public void SubtractValuesTest()
    {
        int x = 10;
        int y = 9;

        MethodsForTesting methods = new MethodsForTesting ();
        int testValue = methods.subtractValues (x, y);

        Assert.True (testValue == 1);
    }

    [Test]
    ```

```
public void MultipleValuesTest()
{
  int x = 9;
  int y = 10;

  MethodsForTesting methods = new MethodsForTesting ();
  int testValue = methods.multiplyValues (x, y);
  Assert.True (testValue == 90);
}

[Test]
public void DivideValuesTest()
{
  int x = 9;
  int y = 3;

  MethodsForTesting methods = new MethodsForTesting ();
  int testValue = methods.divideValues (x, y);
  Assert.True (testValue == 3);
}
```

Running the tests

Now that you have your unit test project in place, you can run the project and examine the results. Perform the following steps to start running the tests:

1. Right-click on the **UnitTests** project and navigate to **Run With | iPhone Retina (3.5-inch) iOS 7.1** (or any other device simulator of your choice).

2. When your simulator opens, you should see the following screen:

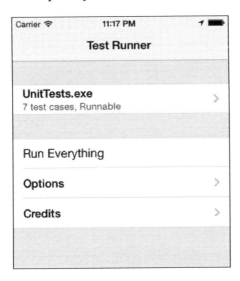

Chapter 7

3. Click the **UnitTests.exe** item and select the **Tests** option. You should see the following screen that lists the available unit tests:

4. If you click `addValuesTests`, `divideValuesTests`, `multipleValuesTests`, or `subtractValuesTests`, you will receive a passing test result. This is shown in the following screenshot:

Testing and Debugging

5. Next, select the **Fail** test option and you will be taken to a screen that explains the failure, including the stack trace information for the error.

6. Finally, return to the main screen and select **Run Everything**.
7. The **UnitTests.exe** item should now include a count of all passing, failing, and ignored tests. If any of the tests have failed or were ignored, then the text will be red; otherwise, it will be green.

How it works

Your test methods each create a new instance of the `MethodsForTesting` class. This introduces an important rule of unit testing. Although this may seem like overkill at first, creating a new instance of the test object for each test maintains the unit structure. You should avoid sharing objects in memory as much as possible when unit testing, because doing so could introduce cascading errors into your test environment which can be notoriously difficult to track down. Once the new object is created, the `Assert` method is called to determine whether the value returned by the method being tested matches the expected value.

> **How do you code the assertion value?**
>
> In the case of our simple tests, it is possible to calculate the expected or assertion value rather than hardcoding it into the code as we have done. Technically speaking, that would be a mistake. Using the .NET arithmetic operators to calculate the assertion value is a bad idea, because we know the methods we are testing are using the exact same arithmetic operators to perform their calculations. Essentially, if an arithmetic operator has a flaw, then the method being tested that uses that operator will have a flaw as well. Nevertheless, the method will still pass the test because both the assertion value and the value returned from the method will be calculated with the same flaw.
>
> So, it's important to ensure that you are using reliable sources for your assertion values. For example, don't try to test a method by comparing its output to itself. That may sound obvious, but I've seen stranger mistakes.

Simulators

Both the iOS and Android platforms provide mechanisms to rapidly test your application in a simulated device environment. As discussed in *Chapter 1, Installing and Setting Up Xamarin Studio*, iOS provides simulators while the Android SDK provides emulators for this purpose, and the two systems are fundamentally different. For more information on those differences, please refer to the *Setting up simulators and emulators* section in *Chapter 1, Installing and Setting Up Xamarin Studio*. For the sake of simplicity, we'll use the term "simulator" to refer to both iOS- and Android-simulated device testing for the remainder of this discussion.

In addition to helping you locate issues and defects in your app during the early phases of development, testing in a simulator provides a number of distinct advantages over physical device testing in several areas. For one, the simulated environment provides testing tools that are not available on the device. For another, simulators can provide basic functionality testing on numerous devices without the need to maintain each of those devices in-house. Also, getting your app deployed to a simulator is typically much faster than deploying it to a device for testing. This is because the physical device deployment process involves several bottlenecks, most notably the transfer process itself. These bottlenecks don't exist when your app is being shuffled around in memory.

Testing and Debugging

This isn't to say that simulator testing alone is sufficient to certify the stability of your app. Simulators have some disadvantages when compared to physical devices as well. Especially in terms of iOS development, a simulator has access to all of the development system's resources. Obviously, this gives the simulator an incredible advantage over its physical counterpart in terms of processing power, memory, and disk space. Although this may seem like a benefit, it's actually a problem if you depend solely on simulator testing, because you'll never know how your app performs in the real world. In fact, the performance difference on the physical device might surprise you in some cases and shock you in others.

Another issue is that a simulator never "gets out of the lab". Physical device testing will allow you to literally take your app out into the real world. If this doesn't seem important to you, try taking your finished map-based application or an application beholden to web service calls into an underground parking garage where there's no network service and see how it performs. Otherwise, if you're feeling particularly bold, leave it up to your end users (that is, paying customers) to find out what happens in that scenario! I'm just guessing here, but you will probably feel the need to implement an offline mode for the Version 1.1.

Therefore, a well-rounded QA program involves both simulated as well as physical device testing. Should you test everything on a physical device? In my opinion, the answer is an emphatic yes! However, that doesn't necessarily mean you should be testing on a physical device every time you tweak your code. As a general rule, the majority of your testing should be performed in a simulator just to confirm that the code is functioning as expected. Then, when you are certain your algorithms and logic are solid, you should follow this up with physical device testing to ensure that the code is as performant as expected.

Exceptions to this rule typically include components that involve the UI, the filesystem, or processes that require large blocks of memory. In these cases, it's better to test on device as early as possible to determine whether your design will even function in the real world before you spend too much time polishing the logic. As strange as it might sound, you will often encounter cases where components work flawlessly in the simulator, only to crash and burn on the device without even showing you the courtesy of providing a decent stack trace.

Testing in an iOS simulator

For this exercise, you're going to create a new iOS solution and perform several basic functions using the simulator. Since you already have experience starting and running the simulator, we're going to focus on those tasks that simulate hardware state changes and user interactions with your View:

1. Create a new solution.

Chapter 7

2. From the **iPhone** group under **iOS**, select the **Empty Project** template.
3. Name your project `iOSInMotion` and click the **OK** button.
4. Right-click on the `iOSInMotion` project and select **Add | New File**.
5. From the iOS group, select **iPhone View Controller** and name your file `MotionViewController`.
6. Replace all of the code in the class declaration with the following code:

```
public MotionViewController () : base ("MotionViewController",
null) { }
public override bool CanBecomeFirstResponder
{
  get
  {
    return true;
  }
}
UILabel label1;

public override void ViewDidLoad ()
{
  base.ViewDidLoad ();
  var frame = new RectangleF (10, 10, 300, 30);
  label1 = new UILabel (frame);
  label1.Text = "I'm just holding a place.";
  View.Add (label1);
}

public override void ViewDidAppear (bool animated)
{
  base.ViewDidAppear (animated);
  this.BecomeFirstResponder();
}

public override void ViewWillDisappear (bool animated)
{
  this.ResignFirstResponder();
  base.ViewWillDisappear (animated);
}

public override void DidReceiveMemoryWarning ()
{
  base.DidReceiveMemoryWarning ();
  label1.Text = "Getting low on memory over here!";
```

Testing and Debugging

```
   }

   public override void DidRotate (UIInterfaceOrientation
      fromInterfaceOrientation)
   {
      base.DidRotate (fromInterfaceOrientation);
      label1.Text = String.Format("WHOA! You just rotated
         me!");
   }

   public override void MotionEnded (UIEventSubtype motion,
      UIEvent evt)
   {
      if (motion == UIEventSubtype.MotionShake)
      {
         label1.Text = "Shake! Shake! Shake!";
      }
   }
}
```

7. Open the `AppDelegate.cs` file.
8. Add the following line of code before the `FinishedLaunching()` method:

   ```
   MotionViewController vc;
   ```

9. Replace the content of the `FinishedLaunching()` method with the following code:

   ```
   UIApplication.SharedApplication.ApplicationSupportsShakeTo
      Edit = true;

   window = new UIWindow (UIScreen.MainScreen.Bounds);
   vc = new MotionViewController ();
   window.RootViewController = vc;
   window.MakeKeyAndVisible ();

   return true;
   ```

Running the tests

Please follow these steps to run the tests:

1. Select either **Debug** or **Release** from the **Build Configuration** dropdown in the toolbar.
2. Select any simulator from the **iOS Simulators** group in the targets' dropdown.
3. Run the application by clicking the **Run** button.

4. Click on the simulator to ensure it has focus.
5. From the menu, select the **Rotate Left** command under **Hardware**.
6. From the menu, select the **Rotate Right** command under **Hardware**.
7. From the menu, select the **Shake Gesture** command under **Hardware**.
8. From the menu, select the **Simulate Memory Warning** command under **Hardware**.
9. From the menu, select the **Home** command under **Hardware**. Your application should transition to the background and you should see the home screen of your simulator.
10. Open your application again from within the simulator.
11. From the menu, select the **Lock** command under **Hardware**. Your screen should go dark, simulating a user locking their device.

How it works

In this exercise, you learned how to mimic physical state changes inside the simulator. Each time the physical state of the simulated hardware changed in some way, the methods inside your MotionViewController class intercepted the event notification from the system and displayed the corresponding message.

Although it isn't possible to demonstrate gestures in action using this very basic application, you can still mimic gestures in the simulator. Reopen the app and hold down the option (*Alt*) key. You will notice two small dots that appear on the screen, as shown in the following screenshot:

Testing and Debugging

These dots indicate that you are now inputting touch events at two separate locations on the screen, which means you can use your touchpad or mouse to mimic gesture motions as though you were using two fingers instead of one. So gestures such as swipe, flick, pinch, two-finger drag, and rotate can be handled through the simulator in the same way as they are handled on the device.

The inputs you tested here are only a few of those available to the iOS simulator platform. You can also use the **Toggle In-Call Status Bar** command to see how your app will look if your user opens it while in a phone call. Also, the **External Displays** command will open an additional window, allowing you to simulate the devices' **TV Out** signal.

> For more information on interacting with the simulator, please check out Apple's iOS Simulator User Guide at `https://developer.apple.com/library/ios/documentation/IDEs/Conceptual/iOS_Simulator_Guide/InteractingwiththeiOSSimulator/InteractingwiththeiOSSimulator.html`.

Testing in an Android emulator

For this exercise, you're creating a new Android solution and performing several basic functions using an Android emulator. Again, your app will focus on handling hardware state changes and user interactions with your Activity:

1. Create a new solution.
2. From the **Android** group, select the **Android Ice Cream Sandwich Application** template.
3. Name your project `AndroidInMotion` and click the **OK** button.
4. Your solution should have opened to the `MainActivity.cs` file. If not, open that file now.
5. Delete this line of code from the `MainActivity.cs` file:
   ```
   Int count = 1;
   ```
6. Replace all of the code in the `OnCreate()` method with the following code:
   ```
   base.OnCreate (bundle);

   var relLayout = new RelativeLayout (this);

   var layoutParams = new RelativeLayout.LayoutParams
     (ViewGroup.LayoutParams.FillParent,
       ViewGroup.LayoutParams.FillParent);
   ```

```
relLayout.LayoutParameters = layoutParams;

var orientation = WindowManager.DefaultDisplay.Rotation;
RelativeLayout.LayoutParams textViewLayoutParams;

if (orientation == SurfaceOrientation.Rotation0 ||
  orientation == SurfaceOrientation.Rotation180)
{
textViewLayoutParams = new RelativeLayout.LayoutParams
  (ViewGroup.LayoutParams.FillParent,
    ViewGroup.LayoutParams.WrapContent);
}
else
{
textViewLayoutParams = new RelativeLayout.LayoutParams
  (ViewGroup.LayoutParams.FillParent,
    ViewGroup.LayoutParams.WrapContent);
textViewLayoutParams.LeftMargin = 100;
textViewLayoutParams.TopMargin = 100;
}

var textView = new TextView (this);
textView.LayoutParameters = layoutParams;
textView.Text = "Programmatically Generated Layout";

relLayout.AddView (textView);

SetContentView (relLayout);
```

Running the tests

Please follow these steps to run the tests:

1. Start your application in **debug** mode. If you haven't done so already, start and run any emulator using **API Level 15 (Ice Cream Sandwich)** or higher.

2. Rotate the device to the left. On a Mac, you need to hold the *fn* and *control* keys, and then click *F11*. On Windows, you can either press *Ctrl* + *F11* or *7* on the numpad.

3. Note the orientation change.

4. Rotate the device to right. On a Mac, you need to hold the *fn* and *control* keys, and then click *F12*. On Windows, you can either press *Ctrl* + *F12* or *9* on the numpad.

How it works

In this exercise, you learned how to simulate physical state changes inside the emulator. As we discussed in *Chapter 6, Application Lifecycle*, Activities are created and destroyed regularly throughout the life of the application object. This process occurs in response to many physical and system events, including whenever the device is rotated. In your application, every time you rotated the emulator the Activity was destroyed and recreated. The same would occur with the Activity running on a physical device.

Android provides an object called the **WindowManager**. Inside the `OnCreate()` method, this object was used to determine the device's current orientation using the `WindowManager.DefaultDisplay.Rotation` property. Using the rotation value as a guide, the `TextView` object was positioned so that it is 100 pixels from the top and the left edges of the screen, and always at the center. The transition is automatically animated as required to give the impression that the objects are only being shifted around, instead of being destroyed and recreated repeatedly.

Note that in this example, you are handling physical state changes programmatically. Android also allows you to handle these declaratively using layout files specific to each orientation. This gives you very specific control over how your Activities will be rendered by the OS under all conditions. However, this control comes at a cost; you actually need to define every Activity twice—once for portrait and once again for landscape mode. Since this effectively doubles the design workload, it's not the ideal workflow in my opinion. There are cases where it will certainly be easier to use the declarative method, but in most cases I would recommend handling these changes programmatically. Of course, do what works best for your project given the requirements and the resources you have available.

Device testing

Now that you are familiar with the fundamentals of simulator testing, let's discuss testing our apps on physical devices. We have already covered how to set up your physical devices for testing in *Chapter 1, Installing and Setting Up Xamarin Studio*, so all that's left is to debug an application on a device from each platform. As discussed earlier in the *Simulators* section of this chapter, you should test all of your functionality on a physical device. That's because the most effective way to certify the behavior and stability of your application is by using it in a real-world environment. If it functions as expected, without crashing, hanging, returning bad values, and so on, then the app is probably ready for release.

Testing on an iOS device

Let's begin with testing on an iOS device.

> If you do not intend to develop iOS applications, or if you do not currently possess a physical iOS device to test on, you may skip this walkthrough for now and come back to it whenever you're ready.

To test on your iOS device, please follow these steps:

1. In Xamarin Studio, open the `iOSInMotion` project you created earlier.
2. Check and ensure that your physical device is connected to your Mac.
3. From the targets' dropdown, select a physical device as a target. This target can have any name, depending on what you called your device. For example, I'm currently using **Will Smith's iPhone** because I save my creativity for designing applications, not naming my devices!
4. Run the application.
5. Once your app is running, take a screenshot by pressing the Home and Sleep buttons at the same time. If your volume is turned up, you will hear the familiar photo click sound effect. In either case, your screen will flash momentarily as the screenshot is saved to your photo roll.

Back on your Mac, open the device with **iTunes** and take a look at the screenshot you just took. Since the app you're using has no code, this is just a blank photo; however, it does confirm that your device is properly configured for running physical tests.

Testing on an Android device

Next, let's perform a test on an Android device.

> If you do not intend to develop Android applications, or if you do not currently possess a physical Android device to test on, you may skip this walkthrough for now and come back to it whenever you're ready.

To test on your Android device, please follow these steps:

1. In Xamarin Studio, open the `AndroidInMotion` project you created earlier.
2. Check and ensure that your physical device is connected to your development machine.

Testing and Debugging

3. From the targets' dropdown, select a physical device as a target. This target can have any name, depending on what you called your device.

4. Run the application.

TestFlight

All of the testing techniques we have discussed up to this point are fine for a single developer or a small team of developers who are working closely with one another. However, what if you have a large team of developers, or what if your team is distributed across the country or even halfway around the world? Or, maybe your project has a dedicated team of testers who don't have access to Xamarin Studio to publish the app to their physical devices.

In the era of virtual offices, remote employees, and flexible schedules, these scenarios are no longer uncommon. Therefore, it's a necessity to have a platform in place to publish the latest development releases to the team in a manner that is efficient. It doesn't hurt if this system is also simple for everyone to use, and not just for the big brains in the development team.

TestFlight is one service that provides this type of platform. TestFlight allows you to publish your apps from within Xamarin Studio, distributing it to all of your team members across the Internet. This service allows you to get your entire team involved with a new release moments after you publish it. Also, it reports crucial metrics such as who has installed the latest version, on which devices, and when they did it. Best of all, at the time of writing this, the service is completely free!

Setting up a TestFlight account

Setting up an account with TestFlight is so simple that I almost hesitate to include it here. However, for the sake of completeness let's walk through it together:

1. Open a browser and navigate to `https://testflightapp.com/register`.

2. Enter your name, e-mail address, and password in the fields provided.

3. Set the **Developer** switch to **ON**.

4. Read the **Terms of Use and Privacy policy** documents via the links provided. If you agree to these terms, check the **I have read and agree** box and click the **Sign Up** button.

5. You're going to land on the welcome screen. Go ahead and click the **Create a New Team** button at this time.

6. Enter your **Team Name** and click the **Save** button.
7. If you wish, you can also move on and invite members to your new team, but that's probably a decision for a later time.

>
>
> **What about all those Android devices?**
>
> TestFlight is great for in-house testing on iOS devices, but the service no longer supports Android devices (as an odd coincidence, this occurred just after Apple bought the parent company). So this begs the question—have you and your testers acquired testing units for each of the Android devices your app could possibly run on? Odds are, you haven't and you don't want to procure and maintain all of those devices in-house due to the cost of purchase and ownership.
>
> This introduces another hardware testing challenge. How do you certify your app is ready for roll-out when you have only been able to test on a percentage of the devices available to consumers? Well, you could just test on the most popular devices and then toss it over the wall, letting your customers find and report any device specific bugs you missed. I politely refer to this method as "letting the market sort it out". Alternatively, there are services available called cloud-based testing.
>
> One example of this is Xamarin's TestCloud, which provides an automatable tool for UI Acceptance Testing using mobile applications in the cloud and using thousands of different physical devices. As a cloud-based service, TestCloud removes the procurement and maintenance costs of these devices from your business, allowing you to focus on your development efforts rather than maintaining a device farm. This service and others like it are not free, but their use allows you to certify the stability of your application with much more confidence than you could if you were only testing on a few devices in-house.

Instruments

Instruments is an analysis and testing tool that comes packaged with Xcode, which you can use to dynamically trace and profile iOS application code. The power and flexibility of this tool cannot be understated as it allows you to track one or more processes and examine the collected data in real time. In addition to the many tools that come packaged in Instruments, you can also create and configure your own custom Instrument tools. Most often, you will find yourself using Instruments to track down and repair memory-related issues. Instruments will not present you with a "quick fix" for memory leaks, but it will remove most of the guesswork.

Testing and Debugging

A detailed discussion of Instruments is beyond the scope of this book. For more information on the tools provided by this suite, please see the documentation on each one at `https://developer.apple.com/library/mac/documentation/developertools/conceptual/instrumentsuserguide/Introduction/Introduction.html`.

Device Monitor

Until recently, the Android SDK didn't provide a suite of analysis tools that offer as many options that are as tightly integrated as Instruments for iOS. However, there is now a package that comes bundled with the SDK called Device Monitor. Device Monitor is also a standalone tool that provides a GUI for a number of Android application debugging and analysis tools. These include **DDMS**, **Tracer for OpenGL ES**, **Hierarchy Viewer**, **Systrace**, **Traceview**, and the **Perfect Pixel Magnification Viewer** tool. You can launch Device Monitor from the SDK's `/tools` folder using the `monitor` command.

A detailed discussion of Device Monitor is beyond the scope of this book. For more information on the tools provided in this suite, check out the documentation on each one at `http://developer.android.com/tools/help/monitor.html`.

Logs

Another invaluable tool for testing purposes is the crash and debug log files generated by your testing platforms. You can learn a tremendous amount of information from a crash log, including the environmental conditions on the device platform when the crash occurred, memory usage of the app, and which library was causing the app to be terminated.

Whenever a crash occurs on an iOS device, the OS will generate a crash log that is then stored to the disk. If your device is synced with iTunes, the log will also be stored on your development machine. Alternatively, you can connect to the device through Instruments and review the crash logs using the diagnostic tools. Viewing the crash logs in Instruments tends to provide a raw picture of what is happening because you will see all of the stack trace information that can be a little difficult to sift through. Often, it's this additional information that gives you the clue you need to pinpoint the source of the problem. If you are looking for crash reports from your end users, you can access those too. If your app was distributed through the iStore, then any crash logs that occur in the field are automatically collected and summarized for you in your iTunes account.

Android device crashes generate debug logs. If you are testing an app on your own device, you can access these logs using the `logcat` command from the console. Even if your device wasn't connected to a build machine when the crash occurred, you can still use the `adb logcat` command to download and review the entire debug log history from the device. If you are looking for debug details from your end users' devices, you can find those in your Google Play developer account also.

Other testing considerations

One last testing concern worth mentioning is the need to take your app offline and get out of the lab. As developers, it's very easy for us to get totally absorbed in our work and forget that outside of our cubicle there is (literally) an entire world. Real-world variables such as poor cell reception, inaccurate GPS reception, and Wi-Fi dead spots can all cause our applications to behave in unpredictable ways if we don't design for these scenarios. You can simulate the offline mode in your simulator by simply turning off the Wi-Fi to OS X and unplugging any network cables, but Wi-Fi isn't the only variable you need to be concerned about.

Therefore, it is extremely important to take the app out from behind the desk as often as you can. For example, I was recently working with a team on a map-based application. While I was working in the office, everything seemed to be going well. GPS accuracy was exceptional, signal strength was off the chart, and Wi-Fi was constantly available. Everything was functioning flawlessly as designed, so we were feeling pretty confident in our work. At lunch one afternoon, I decided to take a walk and carry the app with me for some quick field testing. Before I made it 15 yards from the front door, the Wi-Fi signal dropped off completely and the app promptly locked me out. Oh yeah, offline mode. How did we forget that?

For iOS devices, there are additional location-based simulator tools that you can use from your desk. To access these, while your simulator is running go to the **Location** menu group under **Debug**. Here, you will find several prescripted route files that can simulate significant location changes for your device.

In my opinion, this tool is quite useful to a point. It will confirm whether or not your functions are behaving as expected, and whether your design and logic are correct. However, this is no substitute for actually moving around with the device. For example, outdoor GPS accuracy will vary from location to location, and that accuracy measurement can even "twitch" at times. Additionally, when you first turn a device on the GPS, accuracy can be anywhere from 100 feet to nil. It takes time for the device to pinpoint its location on the planet, and while that is taking place your app could be recording some very inaccurate data. Don't get me wrong, this is a great tool; just don't rely too heavily on it. You still need to test the corner cases and design accordingly.

Summary

We covered a lot of information in this chapter. First, we took a look at the debugging tools that come packaged with Xamarin 3. From there, we examined unit testing options available and reviewed some ideas on how to apply those options. Next, we examined testing on simulators, on emulators, and on physical devices.

After this, we shifted gears to the third-party testing tools that are available for mobile platform developers, and how we can leverage those to improve our development processes and workflows. Tools such as TestFlight can streamline the QA phase of development. Instruments and Device Monitor can help us track down and repair platform-specific memory bugs, while crash and debug logs can be used to help us determine what is happening with our app while it's in the hands of our customers in the real world. Finally, we examined the importance of taking our testing on the road so that we can test how our app behaves under unpredictable scenarios and circumstances.

Unfortunately, this chapter barely scratches the surface of some truly fascinating testing and debugging methodologies. If any of this seems new or strange to you, I would encourage you to take the time to review the references provided in detail. Most of the knowledge in this skill set is universally applicable to all software development platforms and technologies, not just Xamarin 3 and mobile.

In the next chapter, we will look at how to deploy your application through Xamarin Studio and the App Store and Google Play Store.

8
Deployment

In this chapter, we will cover the following topics:

- Deploying iOS applications
- Deploying Mac applications
- Deploying Android applications

Now that your app has been tested, debugged, tested again, hardened, and certified, you're obviously eager to upload it to various marketplaces so that consumers can get their hands on it. I wish I could tell you that the process of deployment to various marketplaces was quick and easy, but there are a number of steps you need to complete to achieve that goal. Additionally, you'll need to carefully plan your deployment and marketing strategy in conjunction with the release schedule so that your app has the best possible chance for being a success. Then, you'll finally be ready to turn over your delicate masterpiece to the review teams for **Gorilla Testing**.

Due to the complicated nature of the deployment process, this chapter is dedicated solely to walking through the procedures of releasing apps to the Apple Store and Google Play Store. For the purpose of these walkthroughs, we are going to release a fictional application called **Ultimate Widget Fu**.

Deploying iOS applications

Let's begin by looking at deploying an iOS application to the App Store.

 If you do not intend to develop iOS applications, or if you are not currently a member of the **iOS Apps Developer Program**, you can skip this walkthrough for now and come back to it whenever you're ready.

Xamarin Studio provides you with the mechanism to publish your app through any of the channels supported by Apple. These include App Store Distribution to the general public, enterprise deployment targeting in-house users, and finally ad hoc deployment for testers. Each of these scenarios requires a corresponding provisioning profile. In this walkthrough, we're going to focus on publishing your app to the App Store.

Before publishing your app, you should take the time to review the **App Store Review Guidelines**. These guidelines will help you avoid the frustration of being rejected for missing something obvious. For example, if your app crashes at any point during execution, it's going to be rejected. Do you plan on mentioning or promoting the Android or Windows Phone versions of your app? Denied. If you try and create an app using the emergency services location-based APIs to track your neighbor's cat, you're going to be shut down. These are just some of the items in the rather lengthy list of nonstarters that Apple has detailed for us.

 Getting rejected is no fun, but it happens to the best of us sometimes. The app reviewers aren't trying to shut your business down; they're just trying to ensure only apps of the highest quality reach the App Store. Whatever you do, don't throw a tantrum on Twitter when this happens, just fix the app.

Knowing the guidelines in advance will minimize the chances of rejection in the first place, so I highly recommend you take time and review the documents found at `https://developer.apple.com/appstore/resources/approval/guidelines.html`.

Distribution provisioning profile

First, you need a **distribution provisioning profile** for your application. This is not the same as the provisioning profile for your device, which was discussed in *Chapter 1, Installing and Setting Up Xamarin Studio*. A distribution provisioning profile, also known as a store provisioning profile, authorizes your app to use the technologies and services that you specified during the development phase. The profile contains a single App ID matching that of your app, plus a distribution certificate. These two components are used to certify that the app was actually submitted to the store by you, which protects both you and your customers.

For iOS apps, you will always need a store provisioning profile in order to submit your app to the App Store. For Mac apps, which we will discuss later, you will only need a store provisioning profile if your app uses technologies and services that require provisioning. Otherwise, you can just use the distribution certificate to sign your app.

Provisioning profiles are generated by the **iOS Provisioning Portal** on the Apple Developer site. In order to complete the generation process, we need the following three things:

- An App ID
- A distribution profile
- A production certificate

The App ID is a two-part string consisting of a **Team ID** and **Bundle ID** that are used to identify one or more applications produced by a single development team. The production certificate is a means of code signing your app so that Apple knows you're the one who created it.

Let's walk through the process of provisioning our application, starting with the production certificate.

Generating a production certificate signing request

Please follow these steps to generate a production certificate signing request:

1. On your Mac, launch **Keychain**.
2. Open the **Preferences...** menu item.
3. Switch to the **Certificates** tab and turn off **Online Certificates Status Protocol (OSCP)** and **Certificates Revocation List (CRL)**.

4. Navigate to **Keychain Access | Certificate Assistant | Request a Certificate from a Certificate Authority…**. Confirm that there are no certificates highlighted in this dialog. If there are, your next request won't be accepted. The following screenshot shows the **Certificate Information** dialog box:

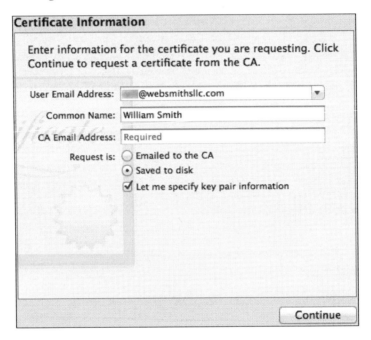

5. In the **User Email Address** field, enter the e-mail address you used when you registered as an iOS developer.
6. Enter your name in the **Common Name** field.
7. Select the **Saved to disk** radio button, and check **Let me specify key pair information**.
8. Click the **Continue** button.

9. Specify a location to save your certificate and click the **Save** button to proceed to the **Key Pair Information** dialog, as shown in the following screenshot:

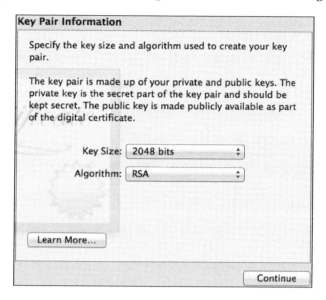

10. For **Key Size**, choose **2048 bits**.
11. For **Algorithm**, choose **RSA**.
12. Click the **Continue** button. Your certificate will be generated and saved to disk.

Submitting a production certificate signing request

Please follow these steps to submit a production certificate signing request:

1. Open a web browser and navigate to http://developer.apple.com.
2. Log in to the **Dev Center**.
3. Click **Member Center** in the navigation bar at the top of the page.
4. Click the **Certificates, Identifiers, and Profiles** button.
5. Under the **Certificates** group, select the **Production** tab.
6. Click the **Add New (+)** button in the upper-right corner.

Deployment

7. Select the **App Store and Ad Hoc** radio button and click the **Continue** button.
8. Click the **Choose File** button that appears on the next screen, and select the certificate file you just generated in Keychain.
9. Click the **Generate** button.
10. Once the **Production Certificate** is generated, click the **Download** button.
11. Open your `Downloads` folder in Finder, and double-click the certificate to install it on your keychain.

Creating the App ID

Please follow these steps to create the App ID:

1. While on the **Certificates, Identifiers, and Profiles** page, select the **Identifiers** group.
2. You will see a list of any currently available **App IDs** attached to your account. To create a new ID, click the **Add New (+)** button in the upper-right corner.
3. Enter a **description** for your app.
4. Choose any **services** your app will require.
5. Select **App ID Prefix**.
6. Enter a unique **Bundle ID** for your app. Apple recommends using a reverse domain style name for this purpose. So in the case of our app, we can enter `com.websmithsllc.ultimatewidgetfu`.
7. Review the information you entered, and if you are satisfied, click the **Submit** button.

Creating and installing the distribution profile

Please follow these steps to create and install the distribution profile:

1. While on the **Certificates, Identifiers, and Profiles** page, select the **Provisioning Profiles** group.
2. You will see a list of any currently available **Provisioning Profiles** attached to your account. To create a new **Provisioning Profile**, click the **Add New (+)** button in the upper-right corner.
3. When prompted, select **App Store** as the **Distribution Method**.
4. Enter a name for this profile. In our case, we will enter `Ultimate Widget Fu`.
5. Click the **Continue** button.

6. Looking at the list of **Distribution Certificates**, ensure that the one you just created is displayed correctly. If so, select that certificate and click the **Continue** button.
7. Select the **App ID** you just created and click the **Continue** button.
8. Name this profile and click the **Generate** button.
9. Once the profile has been generated, click the **Download** button next to the **Distribution Provisioning Profile** you just created, which will download a `.mobileprovision` file.
10. Double-click the `.mobileprovision` file you just downloaded to install the **Distribution Provisioning Profile** to your keychain.

Build configuration

Next, we need to define a new build configuration to be released to the App Store. This build configuration requires the distribution profile you just created. Now that you have that in place, let's walk through adding a new build configuration:

1. Open your solution in Xamarin Studio.
2. Double-click on the solution to open the **Solution Options** dialog.
3. Under the **Build** group, select the **Configurations** panel.
4. Under the **General** tab, click the **Add** button.
5. Name this configuration. Since this configuration will be shared with other solutions in Xamarin Studio, you shouldn't include the solution name here. Choose something more generic such as `Apple` or `AppStore`.
6. Under **Platform**, choose **iPhone**. This might seem like the wrong choice if you are creating a universal application, but the iPhone platform actually represents all iOS applications in this context.
7. Click the **OK** button, and then click the **OK** button again to close the **Solution Options** dialog.
8. Next, double-click the project to open the **Project Options** dialog.
9. Under the **Build** group, select the **iOS Build** panel.
10. Under the **General** tab, set the **Configuration** dropdown to the configuration you just created.

Bundle signing

Please follow these steps for bundle signing:

1. While leaving the **Project Options** dialog open, under the **Build** group, select the **iOS Bundle Signing** pane.
2. Ensure that **Identity** is set to **Distribution (Automatic)**.
3. Xamarin Studio will default to what it thinks is the correct **Provisioning Profile**. This decision is based on the Developer Identity and the Bundle ID. Check to ensure that the selection in this field is correct before continuing.
4. Under the **Build** group, select the **iOS Application** panel.
5. In the **iOS Application** panel under the **iOS Application Target** heading, enter the **Application Name**, **Identifier**, **Version**, and **Target Devices**. Note that the identifier must have the same value that was set for the **Bundle Identifier** when you created your **Provisioning Profile**.
6. If you have not included an **Application Icon** for your app yet, you should do so now under the **iPhone Icons** heading. If your app does not include an **Application Icon**, it will be rejected upon the App Store submission.
7. Click the **OK** button to close the **Project Options** dialog.
8. In Xamarin Studio, set the **Build target** dropdown to the new configuration you just created.
9. Go to **Build** | **Build All** to confirm that no build issues were introduced by the new configuration settings.
10. Once built in the **Release** mode, you should test your app again. As discussed in *Chapter 2, Learning and Customizing the XS Environment*, the **Linker** can have some unintended side effects so it is vital that you test your application's release build before submitting it to the marketplace.

Publishing your application

If your application builds successfully, you're almost ready to submit it to the App Store. Before you do, you're going to need an **iTunes Connect** account. iTunes Connect is the portal to distribute your apps through iTunes, App Store, and more. Through iTunes Connect, you can view the metrics on your app's performance in the field, including any crash logs that are generated by your app when the unthinkable happens. You can also use iTunes Connect to manage the pricing and availability of your app.

Setting up an iTunes Connect account

Let's begin by setting up an account. You can skip this walkthrough if you already have an iTunes Connect account:

1. Begin by opening a web browser and navigating to `https://itunesconnect.apple.com`.
2. Log in with your **Developer Account** credentials.
3. Review the **Terms of Service** agreement. If you agree with the terms, select the checkbox and click the **I Agree** button.

Technically, this is all that is really required to create an iTunes Connect account, assuming you are giving away your apps for free. If you want to get paid for your apps (and who doesn't really?) by selling them or collecting advertising revenue, then you're going to need to complete the **Contracts, Tax and Banking** section. The good news is that this section only needs to be completed once, so it's worth the trouble to go ahead and get it out of the way right now. The bad news is that this section is very lengthy, more than a little bit boring, and its content varies from country to country. For all of these reasons, we're going to leave it out of our discussions here and assume that `Ultimate Widget Fu` is part of a pro bono project.

> For full details of the functionality iTunes Connect provides, please review the Developer Documentation at `https://developer.apple.com/library/ios/documentation/LanguagesUtilities/Conceptual/iTunesConnect_Guide/iTunesConnect_Guide.pdf`.

Creating the application page

Once you have an iTunes Connect account set up, you will need to generate an **App Page** for your app. Before that, there are a few more items you'll need to collect, including:

- **App Name**: This is the name that will appear in the App Store. Note that the text that appears below the **App Icon** following the installation must be derived from the **App Name**. This name has a limit of 255 characters, but that's not an excuse to spam the system with an unnecessarily long name. That being said, you should do some research in advance to learn what keywords people are searching for and, if possible, include one or more of those keywords in your **App Name**. This is one of the most important and often overlooked ways to get more downloads since only the **App Name** and keywords are actually indexed for store searching.

Deployment

- **App Description**: This is the description your users will see in the App Store. There is a limit of 4,000 characters. The first two lines are critical in grabbing the user's attention because Apple will hide the rest behind a **More** link. Be sure your text is clear, concise, and highly scannable. Avoid large blocks of text and try to keep the overall length below 700 characters. This is your chance to sell your app to a customer who is already interested. They want more information, so be sure to put your best foot forward. Focus on functionality, design, and simplicity of workflow from the user's viewpoint. If possible, point out what makes your app unique without naming competitors.

- **App Icon**: You are required to include an **App Icon**, and your app will be rejected without one. The icon should be a 24-bit PNG file with no transparency, and sized 512 x 512 px, or 1024 x 1024 px for Retina displays. Make sure your icon is both memorable and clear, even at a small size. It is also extremely important that the customer can immediately identify the icon from the App Store with the one installed on their device. Remember that this icon is the face of your app, so take the time to design it wisely.

- **App Screenshot**: Screenshots are another often overlooked element for the success of your application. You're required to include at least one app screenshot with your submission, but four more are permitted (and encouraged). You should collect compelling and attractive screenshots, showing the actual screen of your app without borders or graphics around the image. Screenshots are displayed in the order that they are uploaded, and you can't reorder them after the fact. Therefore, always place the best screenshots first because many users will not bother to scroll if the initial screenshots are boring or uninformative. Your screenshots can come in many different shapes, sizes, and resolutions depending on the device and its orientation. For a complete list of the available screenshots and the rules imposed for each, please review *Appendix, Images and Graphics Tables*.

- **App Ratings**: Even if your app isn't targeting children of age 11 or less, it's always a good idea to place ratings on your app to help users make informed decisions. Be aware that Apple will reject any apps that include material determined to be obscene, pornographic, offensive, or defamatory.

At this point, you should have everything you need to begin creating the application page for your app. Although this may feel like a tremendous hassle, the tools provided to you through iTunes Connect via the application page are definitely worth the effort. Plus, you really don't have any other choice. Here's how to create that page:

1. Inside **iTunes Connect**, click the **Managing Your Applications** link.
2. Click the **Add new app** button.
3. If you have multiple developer account types, you will need to specify the **iOS App** type for your new app.

4. Choose the **Primary language** of your app.
5. Enter your company name in the **Company Name** field. Confirm whether your company name is correct before moving on, because once you set this value, it is very difficult to change it later.
6. Fill in your app name in the **App Name** field. Remember that the name appearing under your **App Icon** following the installation must be derived from this value.
7. Enter a SKU number in the **SKU Number** field. The SKU number can be any number with two or more digits.
8. Select your **Bundle ID**. The selections in this dropdown are populated from the **App IDs** you have registered in the **Provisioning Portal**, so be sure you choose the right one for this app.
9. Check your entries one last time. If you are satisfied, click the **Continue** button.
10. Choose the **price tier** for your app. In the case of `Ultimate Widget Fu`, we will choose **Free**. Otherwise, click the **View Pricing Matrix** link to see details on the available options.
11. Click the **Continue** button.
12. On the next screen, begin by entering your **version number** since it is recorded in **Project Options**.
13. Enter the **App Description** you prepared earlier.
14. Select any **categories** that apply to your app.
15. Enter a few **keywords** from the list of keywords you researched earlier while naming your app. This is extremely important because only the **App Name** and this list of keywords are indexed for the App Store search. You should choose keywords that potential users might use to find your app or even a competitor's app. Choose carefully because you can only change this list when you submit an update to your app.
16. Enter your **Copyright information**, which is usually just the release year followed by your company name.
17. Enter your **contact email address**.
18. Enter a **support URL** and any **App URL** for websites that might provide additional information or resources. Note that these websites will also be reviewed by Apple before your app is approved, so remember that many of the rules that apply to your app might also apply to these sites.
19. Enter any **Review Notes**, including additional information the user might need, signup requirements, or hardware requirements.

Deployment

20. Complete the **Rating information** section. Users can change these ratings if they think you've mischaracterized your app, so be as honest as possible.
21. Submit your **graphics**. You will need to upload the **App Icon**, and at least one screenshot. However, if you are submitting a **Universal** app, you will need to submit at least one screenshot for the iPhone and one for the iPad.
22. When these uploads are complete, confirm that you uploaded the right images and click the **Save** button.
23. Click the **View Details** button below the **App Icon**.
24. Click the **Ready to Upload Binary** button.
25. You will be asked whether or not your app uses cryptography or contains incorporate cryptography. Answer honestly and click the **Save** button.
26. Select the availability date for your app. You have two choices for this:
    - If you want your app to be released as soon as it is approved, choose **Automatically release Ultimate Widget Fu 1.0 as soon as it is approved**
    - If you want your app to be released at some time in the future, choose **I will release Ultimate Widget Fu 1.0 after it has been approved**
27. Click the **Save** button.
28. You will be presented with instructions on how to upload your app. Since we will be using Xamarin Studio for this purpose, you can safely ignore these and click the **Continue** button.

Uploading the binary

You will land on your newly created application page. Note that the **Status** of your app page should be listed as **Waiting For Upload**. Now we're going to deploy the app using the **Archive tool** in Xamarin Studio by performing the following steps:

1. Within Xamarin Studio, go to **Build | Archive**.
2. Once the build is completed, the **Archives** tab will open. This tab will display a list of all the archived applications. It's a good idea to select the latest build and add comments. In this case, enter `App Store deployment build`.
3. Open Xcode and go to **Window | Organizer**.
4. Open the **Archives** tab. You will see the same list of archives that you just saw in Xamarin Studio.
5. If you would like to validate your app before submitting it, click the **Validation...** button, which will open **Validation Wizard**.
6. For **method of distribution**, select **Submit to the iOS App Store**.

7. Click the **Next** button.
8. Enter your Apple ID and password so Xcode can log in to iTunes Connect.
9. Click the **Next** button.
10. Once the list of apps with a status of **Waiting For Upload** has been retrieved, you can choose your app page and signing identity from the drop-down lists.
11. Click the **Next** button and Xcode will upload your app.
12. If your app passes validation, you will receive a message stating that no problems were found and your app may be submitted to the App Store.
13. Click the **Distribute...** button, which will open the **Distribution Wizard**. Repeat each of the steps you just performed with the **Validation Wizard**.
14. Once the upload is completed this time, you will receive a message stating it has been submitted to the App Store and is awaiting review.
15. If you open your app page again, the status should be **Waiting For Review**.

You've just submitted your app to the App Store! That wasn't so hard, was it? If everything goes as planned, you should be approved within a few days. Check your app page every day or so until you learn the outcome of the review process. If your app is rejected, a detailed explanation of the rejection will be included for your attention and response. In that case, don't sweat it, just make the changes or fix the bugs as necessary, and submit again.

Deploying Mac applications

Next, let's look at how to deploy Mac applications.

> If you do not intend to develop Mac applications, or if you are not currently a member of the **Mac Apps Developer Program**, you can skip this walkthrough for now and come back to it whenever you're ready.

Mac applications can be distributed in one of the two ways. First, they can be digitally signed by the Developer ID allowing them to be distributed directly to end users without using the App Store. Secondly, if your app has a digitally signed installer package it can be distributed through the App Store. Since the steps required for direct distribution are also required for distribution through the App Store, we will detail both the methods in this walkthrough.

Deployment

Begin by opening a browser and navigating to the Developer Certificate Utility at `https://developer.apple.com/certificates/i`. When you arrive at this page, you will notice four panels listed below the **Mac Developer Program** group. You can view these panels as a checklist, which must be completed to submit your app to the App Store.

Installing Developer Certificates

In order to install your developer certificates, start on the main overview page and perform the following steps:

1. Under **Certificates**, click the **WWDR Intermediate Certificate** link, which will download the certificate. The WWDR Intermediate Certificate is something similar to a root-level certificate authority that checks whether your distribution profile certificate was in fact issued by Apple.

2. Under **Certificates**, click the **Developer ID Intermediate Certificate** link. The Developer ID Intermediate Certificate is used by the Gatekeeper to verify the signed installer.

3. Open your `Downloads` folder in Finder, and double-click the files you just downloaded to install them to your keychain.

Registering a Mac App ID

Just like iOS applications, every Mac application requires a unique App ID:

1. Select the **App ID** panel.

2. If you have never created an App ID previously, you will immediately be taken to the **Register Your Mac App ID** dialog. Otherwise, you will see a list of previously registered **Mac OS X App IDs**. In this case, click the **Create App ID** button in the upper-right corner of the page.

3. Enter a **Name** for your app.

4. Enter a unique **Bundle ID** for your app. Apple recommends using a reverse-domain style name. So in the case of our app, we can enter `com.websmithsllc.ultimatewidgetfu`.

5. Click the **Continue** button.

6. Confirm that the data you have entered is correct because you can't change it later.

7. Click the **Submit** button when you are satisfied.
8. If all goes well, you will be returned to the Mac OS X App IDs list where you will see your new **App ID** listed. From this page, you can set up the **iCloud**, **Push Notifications**, and **Game Center** features by clicking the **Configure** button.

Creating a Mac App Development certificate

A Mac App Development certificate is required if your app needs access to features such as the iCloud or Push Notifications.

> If your Mac application does not utilize these services, you can skip this walkthrough for now and come back to it whenever you need it.

Please follow these steps to create the Mac App Development certificate:

1. Select the **Certificates** panel.
2. Under the **Deployment** category, select the **Mac App Development Certificate** radio button.
3. Click the **Create** button.
4. Open **Keychain** on your Mac.
5. Go to **Keychain Access** | **Certificate Assistant** | **Request a Certificate from a Certificate Authority...**.
6. Inside the **Certificate Information** window, enter the user's e-mail address in the **User Email Address** field.
7. Choose a specific name for the key so you can find it easily later, and enter that value in the **Common Name** field.
8. Select the **Saved to disk** radio button.
9. Click the **Continue** button.
10. This will create a certificate request file with an extension .certSigningRequest on your desktop.
11. Back in **Developer Certificate Utility**, click the **Continue** button.
12. Click the **Choose File** button and locate the .certSigningRequest file you just created.
13. Click the **Generate** button.

14. Once you receive the message that your certificate has been generated, click the **Continue** button again.
15. The next page will list the newly generated certificate including its expiration date. Click the **Download** button.
16. Open your `Downloads` folder in Finder and double-click the certificate to install it to your keychain.
17. Back in **Developer Certificate Utility**, click the **Continue** button.

Creating Mac App Store Certificates

Please follow these steps to create Mac App Store Certificates:

1. Click the **Certificates** panel again.
2. Select the **Mac App Store** radio button.
3. Check both the **Mac App Certificate** and **Mac Installer Certificate** boxes as you will need to create both.
4. Click the **Create** button.
5. Open **Keychain** on your Mac.
6. Go to **Keychain Access | Certificate Assistant | Request a Certificate from a Certificate Authority...**.
7. Inside the **Certificate Information** window, enter the user's e-mail address in the **User Email Address** field.
8. Choose a specific name for the key so that you can find it easily later, and enter that value in the **Common Name** field. Be certain to include the word `Application` in this first key so you can distinguish it later.
9. Select the **Saved to disk** radio button.
10. Click the **Continue** button.
11. This will create a certificate request file with an extension `.certSigningRequest` on your desktop.
12. Back in **Developer Certificate Utility**, click the **Continue** button.
13. Click the **Choose File** button and locate the `.certSigningRequest` file you just created.
14. Click the **Generate** button.
15. Once you receive the message that your certificate has been generated, click the **Continue** button again.
16. The next page will list the newly generated certificate including its expiration date. Click the **Download** button.

17. Open your Downloads folder in Finder and double-click the certificate to install it to your Keychain.
18. Back in **Developer Certificate Utility**, click the **Continue** button once more.
19. You will need to repeat the same process for the **Installer** now. When you name the key, be sure to include the word Installer so you can distinguish it later.
20. Once you have installed these certificates to your keychain, click the **Continue** button to be returned to the **Developer Certificate Utility** main page.

Creating a Developer ID Certificate

Please follow these steps to create a Developer ID Certificate:

1. Click the **Certificates** panel again.
2. Select the **Developer ID** radio button.
3. Check both the **Developer ID Application Certificate** and **Developer ID Installer Certificate** boxes as you will need to create both.
4. Click the **Create** button.
5. From this point, follow the exact same steps that you performed to create **Mac App Store Certificates**, making sure to include the word Application when naming **Developer ID Application Certificate**, and the word Installer when creating **Developer ID Installer Certificate**.
6. Once you have installed these certificates to your keychain, click the **Continue** button to return to the **Developer Certificate Utility** main page.

Registering the Mac OS X development machine

Before you can use the certificates that you just generated to obtain provisioning profiles for your application, you must register the Mac development machine by performing the following steps:

1. Inside **Developer Certificate Utility**, click the **Systems** panel.
2. If you have never created a system previously, you will immediately be taken to the **Register Mac OS X System** dialog. Otherwise, you will see a list of the previously registered **Mac OS X Systems**. In this case, click the **Add Mac OS X System** button in the upper-right corner of the page.

3. In the **System Name or Description** field, enter a descriptive name for the machine you want to register.
4. In the **Hardware UUID** field, enter the **UUID** of this machine. If you are not certain how to find **UUID**, follow the help link provided below the field.
5. Click the **Continue** button.
6. Once the confirmation screen appears, click the **Continue** button.
7. You will be returned to the **Mac OS X Systems** list.

Creating the development provisioning profiles

You must obtain separate provisioning profiles for the development platform and deployed production application. The development provisioning profile is used for local development and testing. Any time you create a new application, or you want to add a new machine to test your application on, you will need to create a new development provisioning profile that associates the App ID with the registered system:

1. Inside **Developer Certificate Utility**, click the **Provisioning Profiles** panel.
2. If you have not created **Mac Development Provisioning Profile** previously, you will immediately be taken to the **Create a Mac Provisioning Profile** dialog. Otherwise, you will see a list of the previously registered Mac Provisioning Profiles. In this case, click the **Create Mac Provisioning Profile** button in the upper-right corner of the page.
3. In the **Kind** group, select the **Development Provisioning Profile** radio button.
4. In the **Name** field, enter the name for this provisioning profile. Be sure to include the word `Development` so you can distinguish it later.
5. Choose the **Mac App ID** that this profile will be associated with.
6. Select the Developer Certificate you created earlier, or whichever certificate you intend to use.
7. Select the system you just registered, or the system you intend to develop and test with.
8. Click the **Create** button.
9. This will generate a new **Development Provisioning Profile**, with the extension `.provisionprofile`. Once the development provisioning profile has been created, click the **Download** button.

10. Navigate to your Downloads folder in Finder, and double-click on the downloaded profile to add it to your Keychain.
11. When prompted, click the **Install** button.

Creating the production provisioning profiles

You must obtain a production provisioning profile before you can submit to the App Store.

1. Inside the **Developer Certificate Utility**, click the **Provisioning Profiles** panel.
2. If you have never created a **Mac Development Provisioning Profile** previously, you will immediately be taken to the **Create Mac Provisioning Profile** dialog. Otherwise, you will see a list of previously registered **Mac Provisioning Profiles**. In this case, click the **Create Mac Provisioning Profile** button in the upper-right corner of the page.
3. In the **Kind** group, select the **Production Provisioning Profile** radio button.
4. In the **Name** field, enter the name for this provisioning profile. Be sure to include the word Production so you can distinguish it later.
5. Choose the **Mac App ID** that this profile will be associated with.
6. Select the **Mac App Certificate** you created earlier, or whichever certificate you intend to use.
7. Click the **Create** button.
8. This will generate a new **Production Provisioning Profile**, with the extension .provisionprofile. Once the production provisioning profile has been created, click the **Download** button.
9. Navigate to your Downloads folder in Finder, and double-click on the downloaded profile to add it to your keychain.
10. When prompted, click the **Install** button.

Setting the app configuration

The last step needed to prepare for the release build is to set up our application configuration:

1. Open your solution in Xamarin Studio.
2. Right-click the project and open the **Project Options** dialog.
3. Under the **Build** group, select the **Mac OS X Application** panel.
4. Choose **App Icon**.

Deployment

5. In the **Application Category** dropdown, specify the app category.
6. In the **Identifier** field, enter the **Bundle ID** you defined when you created the **App ID**.
7. Define the **Version** and **Build** values.
8. Choose **Deployment Target**. This is the minimum OS level that will run your app.
9. Choose **Main Interface**.
10. Under the **Build** group, select the **Mac OS X Packaging** panel.
11. In the **General** tab, check the **Include the Mono runtime in the application bundle** box. Embedding the mono runtime is a requirement for the App Store submission.

Signing your application for direct deployment

At this stage, you should be ready to deploy your app, and this is where the workflow paths diverge. If you are planning to deploy your app directly to your customers, you should sign your app using your Developer ID and then build for release. I say you should sign your app because technically it's not required. The gatekeeper will not immediately permit an unsigned app to be installed, but users can bypass that restriction. The exact procedure to bypass the security will differ from OS version to version, but just be aware that it's possible.

> If allowing users to install your app outside of the security protection of Gatekeeper fits with your development and deployment workflow, you can skip these steps.
>
> If you do not intend to deploy your applications directly to users, opting instead to deploy via the Mac App Store, you can skip the next section as well.

Please use the following steps to sign your application for direct deployment:

1. Back in the **Project Options** dialog under the **Mac OS X Packaging** panel, change the **Configuration** to **Release**.
2. In the **General** tab, under the **Code Signing Options** heading, check the **Sign the application bundle** box.
3. Choose your **Developer ID** from the **Identity** dropdown.

4. Choose your **Production Provisioning Profile** from the **Provision** dropdown.
5. Under the **Packaging Options** heading, check both the **Create installer package** and **Sign the installer package** boxes.
6. Choose your **Developer ID** from the remaining **Identity** dropdown.

Build for direct deployment

At this time, your app is ready for a release build intended for direct deployment:

1. Close the **Project Options** dialog.
2. Choose the **Release | x86** configuration from the **Configuration** dropdown.
3. Go to **Build | Build All** to confirm that no build issues were introduced using the new configuration settings.
4. During the build process, you will be prompted twice to **Allow your Developer ID certificate to be used** for signing the build package.
5. Once built in the **Release** mode, you should test your app again, this time by installing it locally using the newly created package. As discussed in *Chapter 2*, *Learning and Customizing the XS Environment*, the **Linker** can have some unintended side effects so it is vital that you test your application's release build before submitting it to the marketplace. Also, you want to ensure that the installer is working as you intend.
6. You will find the `.pkg` file located in the `bin/Release` folder of your solution.

You have now successfully created an installer package that can be directly distributed to your end users!

Signing your application for deployment to the Mac App Store

If you are planning to deploy your app via the Mac App Store, you will be required to sign your app using your Developer ID and then build for release. The next two sections will walk you through signing and building your app for that purpose.

> If you do not intend to deploy your applications via the Mac App Store, opting instead to deploy directly to your users, you can skip the remainder of the Deploying Mac applications walkthrough.

Deployment

Please use the following steps to sign your application for deployment to the Mac App Store:

1. Back in the **Project Options** dialog under the **Mac OS X Packaging** panel, change the **Configuration** to **AppStore**.
2. In the **General** tab, under the **Code Signing Options** heading, check the **Sign the application bundle** box.
3. Choose your **Developer ID** from the **Identity** dropdown.
4. Choose your **Production Provisioning Profile** from the **Provision** dropdown.
5. Under the **Packaging Options** heading, check both the **Create installer package** and **the Sign the installer package** boxes.
6. Choose your **Developer ID** from the remaining **Identity** dropdown.

Build for Mac App Store deployment

At this time, your app is ready for release build for direct deployment.

1. Close the **Project Options** dialog.
2. Choose the **AppStore** configuration from the **Configuration** dropdown.
3. Go to **Build | Build All** to confirm that no build issues were introduced using the new configuration settings.
4. During the build process, you will be prompted at two different points to **Allow your Developer ID certificate to be used for signing** the build package.
5. Once built in the **AppStore** mode, you should test your app again, this time by installing it locally using the newly created package. As discussed in *Chapter 2, Learning and Customizing the XS Environment*, the **Linker** can have some unintended side effects so it is vital that you test your application's release build before submitting it to the marketplace. Also, you want to ensure that the installer is working as you intend.
6. You will find the `.pkg` file located in the `bin/x86/AppStore` folder of your solution.

You have successfully created an installer package that can be uploaded to the Mac App Store!

Deploying to the Mac App Store

Just like iOS applications, you will use iTunes Connect to deploy applications to the Mac App Store. For details on setting up an iTunes Connect account, please review the *Setting up an iTunes Connect account* section earlier in this chapter. Likewise, before you can continue on to publishing your app, there are a few more items you will need to define or collect. You will find that most of these items are similar to their iOS counterparts:

- **App Name**: This is the name of the app that will appear in the App Store, and it has a limit of 255 characters. You should do some research in advance to learn what keywords people are searching for and, if possible, include one or more of those keywords in your **App Name**. This is one of the most important and often overlooked ways to get more downloads.

- **App Description**: This is the description your users will see in the App Store. There is a limit of 4,000 characters. The first two lines are critical in grabbing the user's attention because Apple will hide the rest behind a **More** link. Be sure your text is clear, concise, and highly scannable. Avoid large blocks of text, and try to keep the overall length below 700 characters. This is your chance to sell to a customer who has already taken the time to look for more information. Focus on functionality, design, and simplicity of workflow from the user's viewpoint. If possible, point out what makes your app unique without naming competitors.

- **App Screenshot**: Screenshots are another often overlooked element for the success of your application. You must include at least one app screenshot with your submission, but four more are permitted (and encouraged). You should collect compelling and attractive screenshots, showing the actual screen of your app without borders or graphics around the image. Screenshots are displayed in the order they are uploaded, and you cannot reorder them after the fact. Always place the best screenshots first because many users will not bother to scroll if the initial screenshots are boring or uninformative. For a complete list of the available screenshots and the rules imposed for each, please review *Appendix, Images and Graphics Tables*.

- **App Ratings**: Even if your app isn't targeting children of age 11 or less, it's always a good idea to place ratings on your app to help users make informed decisions. Note that Apple will reject any apps that include material determined to be obscene, pornographic, offensive, or defamatory.

Deployment

At this point, you should have everything you need to begin creating the application page for your app. Here's how to create that page:

1. Inside iTunes Connect, click the **Managing Your Applications** link.
2. Click the **Add new app** button.
3. If you have multiple developer account types, you will need to choose the **Mac OS X App** type.
4. Choose the **primary language** of your app.
5. Fill in your app name in the **App Name** field.
6. Enter a SKU number in the **SKU Number** field. The SKU number can be any number with two or more digits.
7. Select your **Bundle ID**. The selections in this dropdown are populated from the **App IDs** you have registered in the **Provisioning Portal**, so be sure you choose the right one for this app.
8. Check your entries one last time. If you are satisfied, click the **Continue** button.
9. Select the availability date for your app. You have two choices for this:
    - If you want your app to be released as soon as it is approved, choose today's date.
    - If you want your app to be released at some time in the future, choose a date that you are certain of after the review process will finish, perhaps a year from now. Then, once approved, you can deploy the app on your schedule.
10. Choose the price tier for your app. In the case of `Ultimate Widget Fu`, we will choose **Free**. Otherwise, click the **View Pricing Matrix** link to see details on the available options.
11. Click the **Continue** button.
12. On the next screen, begin by entering your version number as it is recorded in your **Project Options**.
13. Enter your copyright information, which is usually just the release year followed by your company name.
14. Select any categories that apply to your app.
15. Complete the **Rating** information section. Users can change these ratings if they think you mischaracterized your app, so be as honest as possible.
16. Enter the **App Description** you prepared earlier.

17. Enter a few keywords from the list of keywords you researched earlier while naming your app. Just as in the case of iOS apps, this is extremely important because only the app name and this list of keywords are indexed for the App Store search.

18. Enter a marketing URL and privacy policy URL if they are available. Note that these websites will also be reviewed by Apple before your app is approved, so remember that many of the rules that apply to your app might also apply to these sites.

19. Enter your contact information including your first name, last name, e-mail address, and phone number.

20. Enter any **Review Notes**, including additional information the user might need, signup requirements, or hardware requirements.

21. If your application has a **Demo** mode, enter the account credentials under the **Demo Account Information** heading.

22. If your app uses any entitlements, enter the necessary keys in the table under the **App Sandbox Entitlement Usage Information** heading.

23. Finally, under the **Uploads** heading, you should add your screenshots. You will need to upload at least one screenshot.

24. When these uploads are complete, confirm that you selected the right images and click the **Save** button.

25. Click the **View Details** button below the **App Icon**.

26. In the **View Details** dialog, click the **Ready to Upload Binary** button.

27. You will be asked whether or not your app uses cryptography or contains incorporate cryptography. Answer honestly and click the **Save** button.

28. You will be advised that **iTunes Connect** is ready to accept your binary file. Click the **Continue** button.

29. This will open the **Start Application Loader** tool. Once you are logged in, click the **Deliver Your App** button to proceed.

30. Choose your application from the dropdown, and click the **Next** button.

31. Review the data associated with your application. If everything looks correct, click the **Next** button.

32. When Finder opens, you will find the binary in the solution's directory under the `bin/x86/AppStore` folder. Select the file and click the **Open** button.

33. Click the **Send** button.

34. At this time, the package will be validated. Your package will be submitted for review if no errors are found. Otherwise, fix the errors that are reported and upload again.

Deployment

You've just submitted your Mac app to the App Store! If everything goes as planned, you should be approved within a few days. Check the app page every day or until you learn the outcome of the review process. If your app is rejected, a detailed explanation of the rejection will be included for your attention and response. Make the required changes or fix the bugs as necessary, and submit your app again.

Deploying Android applications

Deploying an Android application includes many of the same steps you took to deploy an iOS or Mac application. One noteworthy difference is that while iOS apps can only be distributed via the iOS App Store, there are many modes of deployment for your Android apps. These include the big app stores such as Google Play Store and Amazon App Store for Android, other lesser known app stores, independent outlets, or your own website. It's even possible to release your app by e-mail, although I don't know anyone personally who has ever done this.

Although publishing an app through an established marketplace requires additional effort on your part, these outlets really do provide access to the greatest number of potential customers within your target market. Plus, you can deploy to multiple markets simultaneously to increase your market exposure quickly. For the purpose of this demonstration, we're going to focus on deployment to what is still the most prominent marketplace, the Google Play Store.

Preparing your application for release compile

First, you need to build your application in the **Release** mode. To do so, please follow these steps:

1. Open your application solution in Xamarin Studio.
2. Open the `Project/AssemblyInfo.cs` file.
3. You need to disable debugging to prevent outside applications from taking control of your Java process and executing additional code in the context of your application. The best way to do this is to simply add the following preprocessor directive to the `AssemblyInfo.cs` file:

   ```
   #if DEBUG
   [assembly: Application(Debuggable=true)]
   #else
   [assembly: Application(Debuggable=false)]
   #endif
   ```

Chapter 8

4. Double-click the project to open the **Project Options** dialog.
5. Under the **Build** group, select the **Android Application** panel.
6. Select an application icon for your app. The icon should be 512 x 512 px, 32-bit PNG format. Transparency is allowed, but the maximum file size must not exceed 1024 KB. The application icon is extremely important because some marketplaces, including the Google Play Store, will not permit your app to be listed without it.

>
> Note that if you are building your app using the Visual Studio plugin, you will not be able to set this value in the **Project Options** dialog. Therefore, you must edit the `Project/AssemblyInfo.cs` file directly. Insert the following code snippet into the `AssemblyInfo.cs` file. Remember to replace `iconName` with the actual name of your icon file:
> `[assembly: Application(Icon = "@drawable/iconName")]`

7. While still inside the **Android Application** panel, set the **Version number** value. This value is used internally by Android and the application to determine when to apply available updates. Most applications on their initial release begin by setting this value to 1, and then incrementing from there by whatever system you have chosen. Interestingly, I once worked for a company that "does not release 1.0 Versions" of its software, so all of their initial releases were labeled as 2.0 and above. If you have similar concerns about the consumer's perception of your products, don't worry because the **Version number** is never seen by the user.

8. Next, set the **Version name**. This value is not used in any way by the system, but is instead used to communicate information to your end user. For an initial release, it would be appropriate (but not required) to enter a value of 1.0 in this field.

9. Under the **Build** group, select the **Android Build** panel.

10. Change the **Configuration** mode to **Release**. This is important because the **Release** mode turns off the shared runtime, excludes debugging components, and activates the **Linker**, which will discard any assemblies, types, and members that are not referenced by your project. All of these result in a much leaner **APK**, or **Android Application Package file**. Keeping the APK lean is important because the Google Play Store imposes a 50 MB file size limit on the APK.

11. Build your application to ensure that none of the changes have broken your solution. Once your app is built in the **Release** mode, you should test your app again.

[209]

Creating a private keystore

Android will not execute applications that have not been digitally signed. A digital signature includes the application creator's identity, and assures the OS that the app was created by a trustworthy source. Signing your APK requires a keystore, which is a database containing security certificates created by the `keytool` program in the Java SDK. Once created, these certificates must be stored in a place where the signing tool can access them.

Keep your keystore safe!

It is vitally important that you maintain your keystore in a safe and reliable repository! If you lose the keystore, you won't be able to post updates to your application within the Google Play Store. Your only course of action would be to delete the old application from the marketplace, create a new keystore, resign the APK with the new key, and then submit a completely new application.

Another concern is security. If the keystore is compromised, it would be possible for a hacker to distribute uncertified code under the name of your application, including malicious versions of your app. Obviously, this kind of breach can be very bad for business!

To create a new private keystore, you must complete the following steps:

1. Open a terminal session on your Mac. If you are on a Windows machine, open a command console.
2. The `keytool` utility comes with the JDK, so you will be able to launch it from the directory that contains `javac`. If you're not sure where that directory is, please refer to the tip at the end of this section.
3. Use the following code snippet to execute `keytool`. Remember to replace `fileName` with the intended filename for your keystore, and `keyName` with the name of the key you want to create inside the store:

   ```
   keytool -genkey -v -keystore fileName.keystore -alias
      keyName -keyalg RSA -keysize 2048 -validity 10000
   ```

4. When prompted, enter the **keystore password**.
5. When prompted again, re-enter the **keystore password**.
6. Answer the series of security questions that are presented.
7. When prompted, enter the password for the key name if it is different than that of the keystore.
8. When prompted, re-enter the password for the key name.

> **Where is the keytool?**
>
>
> Finding the keytool can be a pain if you're not sure where to look. On either a Windows machine or a Mac, a keytool is bundled with the Java SDK so it's available in the same directory that contains `javac`. On a Windows machine, that directory is always located at `%JAVA_HOME%\bin`.
>
> If you're not sure where `%JAVA_HOME%` points towards, check your system's environment variables to confirm the directory.
>
> Locating the bin path on a Mac is also very simple. Open a terminal and enter the following command:
>
> `cd `/usr/libexec/java_home`/bin`
>
> Note that in the preceding code, the quotes are back ticks, not normal single quotes.

Signing the APK

There are several ways to sign the APK. In our case, we're going to sign it through Xamarin Studio. There are different sets of steps involved with signing the APK using the Visual Studio plugin, but we will not detail them here. Perform the following steps to sign the APK:

1. With your solution open in Xamarin Studio, go to **Project** | **Publish Android Application...**.
2. In the **Keystore selection** dialog, choose the keystore you just created from the **Location** field.
3. Enter the password for the keystore in the **Password** field.
4. Reenter the **password** for the keystore in the **Confirm** field.
5. In the **Alias** field, enter the **key-name** you chose when you ran `keytool`.
6. Enter the **key-name password** in the **Key password** field.
7. Click the **Forward** button.
8. In the **Select destination** dialog, enter a target directory for the signed APK.
9. Enter the APK name in the **File** field.
10. Click the **Create** button.

At this stage, you have a signed APK file that is ready for deployment.

Deployment

Publishing to the Google Play Store

Before you can publish your app to the Google Play Store, there are a few more items you will need to collect:

- **App Name**: This is the name of the app that will appear in the Google Play Store. The Google Play Store imposes a 30-character limit on your **App Name**! As with an iOS app, you should do some research in advance to learn what keywords people are searching for and, if possible, include one or more of those keywords in your **App Name**.

- **App Description**: This is the description your users will see in the App Store. There is a limit of 4,000 characters here. The first two lines are critical in grabbing the user's attention. Be clear, concise, and highly scannable. Avoid large blocks of text, and try to keep the overall length below 700 characters. This is your chance to sell to a customer who has already taken the time to look for more information. Focus on functionality, design, and simplicity of workflow from the user's viewpoint. If possible, point out what makes your app unique without naming.

- **Category**: Choosing a category is a requirement for apps distributed via the Google Play Store. Be honest, as choosing an inappropriate category can result in your app being removed.

- **Application Type**: You must choose either **Application** or **Game**. Hopefully, by this stage you already know the answer to this question!

- **Company Name**: You must include your company name with your app submission to the Google Play Store. If you haven't picked one out, now's the time.

- **Support Information**: An e-mail address, URL, or phone number for providing user support is required for apps submitted to the Google Play Store. You must include one or more of these values.

- **Launcher Icons**: You should include launcher icons for each of the generalized screen densities, including 36 x 36 px for ldpi (120dpi), 48 x 48 px for mdpi (160dpi), 72 x 72 px for hdpi (240dpi), and 96 x 96 px for xhdpi (320dpi). These images must be a 32-bit PNG file and transparency is allowed.

- **Additional Graphics**: You have the option to include two additional graphics, titled **Promo Graphic** and **Feature Graphic**. The **Promo Graphic** must be 180 x 120 px, 24-bit PNG, with no border and no transparency. The **Feature Graphic** can be up to 1024 x 500 px, but to be on the safer side, you should stay within a 924 x 400 px frame. The graphic must also be 24-bit PNG with no transparency. Google officially states that the promo and feature graphics are optional, but you should really consider them a requirement. These graphics are used whenever your app is featured anywhere in the App Store, and their inclusion can greatly enhance your app page.
- **App Screenshot**: Screenshots are another often overlooked element for the success of your application. You must include at least two app screenshots with your submission for each supported device platform, including phones, 7-inch tablets, and 10-inch tablets. However, six more screenshots are permitted (and encouraged) for each platform, allowing a total of eight screenshots per platform (24 in all). You should collect compelling and attractive screenshots, showing the actual screen of your app without borders or graphics around the image. Always place the best screenshots first because many users will not bother to scroll if the initial screenshots are boring or uninformative. Your screenshots can come in many different shapes, sizes, and resolutions depending on the device and its orientation. You should, at a minimum, include a portrait screenshot in 320 x 480 px, 480 x 800 px, and 480 x 854 px sizes. Note that landscape screenshots will be cropped. For a complete list of the available screenshots and the rules imposed for each, please review *Appendix, Images and Graphics Tables*.
- **Video Link**: You can also include a link to a YouTube video demonstrating your application's functionality. This video should be 30 seconds to 2 minutes in length. Although it is optional, I highly recommend including a video if you have the means to do so. Nothing can communicate both the functionality and simplicity of your app workflow like a demonstration.

Once you have these materials in hand, you are ready to upload the APK to the Google Play Store:

1. Open a web browser and log in to the **Google Play Developer Console**.
2. Click the **Publish App on Google Play** button.
3. Click the **All Applications** group on the left.
4. Click the **Add new application** button.
5. Choose a default language.

6. Enter a name for your application in the field provided.
7. Click the **Upload an APK** button.
8. Click the **Upload your first APK to Production** button.
9. Click the **Browse** button and select your **signed APK file**. The widget will automatically upload and assess your file to ensure that it is a valid APK file.
10. Once complete, you will see your app listed on the **Production** tab with a status of **Draft in Production**.
11. Click the **Save Draft** button.
12. Click the **Store Listing** tab.
13. Enter your app's title, description, and promo text (optional) in the respective fields.
14. Using the widget under the **Graphics Assets** header, upload your icons and screenshots.
15. Add a link to your promotional video in the **Promo Video** field.
16. Under the **Categorization** header, choose **Application Type**, **Category**, and **Content rating**.
17. Under the **Contact Details** header, enter your **support information**.
18. Enter a **URL** to your **privacy policy** (optional).
19. Click the **Pricing and Distribution** tab.
20. If you intend to publish paid applications or you want to provide in-app products, you will need an active merchant account. The process of opening a merchant account is lengthy and varies by country so I will leave it up to you to complete that later.
21. Select any countries you wish to distribute your app to.
22. Scroll down to the **Consent** section.
23. Read the links on **Content guidelines** and **US export laws**. If you understand and acknowledge/consent to these, check the boxes. Your selections will be automatically saved.
24. If for some reason you see a **Draft** button in the upper-right corner of the page, it means there is a problem with your submission. Otherwise, you should see the **Ready to publish** button in the upper-right corner. Click that button, and choose the **Publish this app** option from the subsequent dropdown.

That's it! Your application has been published and it should be available in the Google Play Store within a few hours.

Summary

In this chapter, we have walked through the process of taking our finished applications from the development department to the open market. Although these processes are lengthy and cumbersome in places, they help to ensure that only the highest quality products are available to customers using the various marketplaces. This translates to a more positive experience for users of the marketplace, which in turn means increased trust in the marketplace system and its vendors as a whole.

Images and Graphics Tables

The following sections contain lists and tables of the image and graphics specifications that we will require while working on our app.

iOS application icons

The following list and table show specifications and requirements for iOS application icons:

- File Type: PNG
- Quality: 24 bit
- Transparency: Not allowed
- Required: Yes

Type	Dimensions (px)	Notes
Standard	512 x 512 px	
Retina	1024 x 1024 px	

iOS 3.5-inch Retina display screenshots

The following list and table show specifications and requirements for iOS screenshots for 3.5-inch Retina displays:

- File Type: High-quality JPEG, TIFF, or PNG
- Quality: 72 dpi, RGB, flattened
- Transparency: Not allowed
- Required: At least one

Type	Dimensions (px)	Notes
Portrait	640 x 920	Hi-res, do not include status bar
Portrait	640 x 960	Hi-res, fullscreen
Landscape	960 x 600	Hi-res, do not include status bar
Landscape	960 x 640	Hi-res, fullscreen

iOS 4-inch Retina display screenshots

The following list and table show specifications and requirements for iOS screenshots for 4-inch Retina displays:

- File Type: High-quality JPEG, TIFF, or PNG
- Quality: 72 dpi, RGB, flattened
- Transparency: Not allowed
- Required: At least one screenshot is required if your app will run on 4-inch Retina displays and up to four additional screenshots are permitted

Type	Dimensions (px)	Notes
Portrait	640 x 1096	Do not include status bar
Portrait	640 x 1136	Fullscreen
Landscape	1136 x 600	Do not include status bar
Landscape	1136 x 640	Fullscreen

iOS iPad screenshots

The following list and table show specifications and requirements for iOS application screenshots for iPad:

- File Type: High-quality JPEG, TIFF, or PNG
- Quality: 72dpi, RGB, flattened
- Transparency: Not allowed
- Required: At least one screenshot is required if your app will run on an iPad and up to four additional screenshots are permitted

Type	Dimensions (px)	Notes
Portrait	768 x 1004	Do not include status bar
Portrait	768 x 1024	Fullscreen
Portrait	1536 x 2008	Hi-res, do not include status bar
Portrait	1536 x 2048	Hi-res, fullscreen
Landscape	1024 x 748	Do not include status bar
Landscape	1024 x 768	Fullscreen
Landscape	2048 x 1496	Hi-res, do not include status bar
Landscape	2048 x 1536	Hi-res, fullscreen

Mac OS X app screenshots

The following list and table show specifications and requirements for Mac OS X application screenshots:

- File Type: High-quality JPEG, TIFF, or PNG in the RGB color space
- Quality: 72dpi, RGB, flattened
- Transparency: Not allowed
- Required: At least one screenshot is required and up to four additional screenshots are permitted

Type	Dimensions (px)	Notes
	1280 x 800	16:10 aspect ratio
	1440 x 900	16:10 aspect ratio
	2880 x 1800	16:10 aspect ratio

Android application icons

The following list and table show specifications and requirements for Android application icons:

- File Type: PNG
- Quality: 32 bit
- Transparency: Allowed
- Required: Yes

Type	Dimensions (px)	Notes
Standard	512 x 512 px	1024 KB maximum file size

Android screenshots

The following list and table show specifications and requirements for Android application screenshots:

- File Type: JPG or PNG
- Quality: 24 bit
- Transparency: Not allowed
- Required: At least two screenshots are required for each supporting device platform, including phones, 7-inch tablets, and 10-inch tablets, and up to six additional screenshots are permitted (all screenshots should be in the portrait mode)

Type	Dimensions (px)	Notes
Screenshots	Min: 320 Max: 3840	Maximum dimension cannot be more than twice as long as the maximum dimension.
Feature Graphic	1024 x500	The Feature Graphic is used for promotions on Google Play.
Promo Graphic	180 x 120	The Promo Graphic is used for promotions on older versions of the Android OS (earlier than 4.0). A promo graphic is optional.

Index

A

Actions
  about 80, 81
  adding 82
active state, iOS application lifecycle 145
Add-on Sites Manager, Android SDK Manager 93
Ad-Hoc Provisioning Profile 64
Advanced tab, Android Build pane
  options 66
Advanced tab, iOS Build pane
  options 63
Android Activity 120
Android Activity lifecycle methods
  OnCreate() 153
  OnDestroy() 154
  OnPause() 154
  OnRestart() 153
  OnResume() 153
  OnStart() 153
  OnStop() 154
Android application
  creating 42
Android application deployment
  APK, signing 211
  application, building in
    Release mode 208, 209
  performing 208
  private keystore, creating 210
  publishing, to Google Play Store 212-214
Android application icons 220
Android application lifecycle
  about 150
  Activity lifecycle, examining 156, 157
  Activity lifecycle methods 152, 153
  application states, examining 155, 156
  background state 151, 157, 158
  configuration change 155
  empty state 151
  foreground state 150
  service state 151
  visible state 150
Android Build pane
  Advanced tab 66, 67
  Linker tab 65
  Packaging tab 64
Android Developer Library 37
Android device
  testing 177
Android devices, setting up
  about 33
  debugging, enabling on device 33
  USB drivers, installing 34
Android emulator
  about 22
  testing in 174
  tests, running 175
  working 176
Android Fragment file type
  using 120
Android Layouts 94, 95
Android project templates
  about 113
  Android Application 113
  Android Honeycomb 113
  Android Ice Cream Sandwich 113
  Android Library 114
  Android OpenGL Application 114
  Android Unit Test 114
  Android WebView 114
  Java Bindings Library 114

Android screenshots 220
Android SDK Manager
  about 92
  Add-on Sites Manager 93
  AVD Manager 94
  Package Manager 92, 93
Android View 120
Android Virtual Device (AVD) 21
Andr.Unit framework 164
API design, Xamarin.Forms
  about 126
  using 126-132
APK
  signing 211
APM EABI v7a System Image 26
AppDelegate class
  DidEnterBackground() function 146
  FinishedLaunching() function 146
  OnActivated() function 145
  OnResignActivation() function 146
  WillEnterForeground() function 146
  WillFinishLaunching() function 146
  WillTerminate() function 146
AppDelegate object 145
App Fundamentals tutorial
  URL 37
Apple Developer Library
  URL 37
Apple Developer Program
  about 17, 18
  iOS Developer Program account 17
  Mac Developer Program 17
Apple support documentation
  URL 12
Application Binary Interface (ABI) 66
application lifecycles
  Android application lifecycle 150
  iOS application lifecycle 144
Application menu
  about 46-48
  About Xamarin Studio 46
  Account... 47
  Add-in Manager... 47
  Check for updates... 46
  Custom Policies... 47
  Preferences... 46

App Page, iOS application
  App Description 192
  App Icon 192
  App Name 191
  App Ratings 192
  App Screenshot 192
  creating 191-194
App Store Review Guidelines 184
ARC (automatic reference counting) 86
Attributes inspector 78
AVD Manager
  about 94
  used, for creating Nexus 7 AVD 22, 23
AVD performance
  Hardware Acceleration
    Execution Manager 27
  improving 26
  Intel x86 Atom System Image 26, 27
  running, from Snapshot 29
  third-party AVD options 30

B

background state, Android application
    lifecycle 157, 158
background state, iOS application
    lifecycle 145
Basic Input/Output System (BIOS) 28
Binding Project
  about 116
  iOS Binding Project 116
  Java Bindings Library 117
Blank App (Xamarin.Forms Portable) 124
Blank App (Xamarin.Forms Shared) 124
breakpoint navigator 77
build configuration, iOS application
  defining 189
Build group, Project Options
  Android Build pane 64
  iOS Build pane 61
Build menu
  about 51-53
  Build 51
  Clean 52
  Rebuild 51
  Stop 52

Bundle ID 185
Business edition, Xamarin Studio 9

C

Class Library (Xamarin.Forms Portable) 124
cloning 22
collection view cells 119
collection view controllers 119
components, Xamarin.Forms
  about 125
  Cell 126
  Layout 126
  Page 126
  View 126
connections inspector 78
continuous integration (CI)
  about 163
  URL 163

D

data bindings, Xamarin.Forms 125
debug area, Xcode 79
debugging 162
debug navigator 77
deployment
  Android applications 208
  iOS applications 184
  Mac applications 195
DESIGNER files 85
Design pads 43, 44
developer certificates, Mac application
  installing 196
Developer Certificate Utility
  URL 196
Developer ID Certificate, Mac application
  creating 199
development components
  installing 11
development provisioning profiles, Mac application
  creating 200
Device Monitor
  about 161, 180
  launching 180

URL 180
device testing
  about 176
  Android device, testing 177
  iOS device, testing 177
Dialog View Controller (DVC) 119
DidEnterBackground() function 146
direct deployment, Mac application
  build 203
  signing for 202
distribution provisioning profile, iOS application
  about 185
  App ID, creating 188
  creating 188
  installing 189
  production certificate signing request, generating 185-187
  production certificate signing request, submitting 187, 188
  requisites, for generation process 185
D-U-N-S Numbers 18

E

Edit menu
  about 46-48
  Insert Standard Header 48
  Insert Template... 48
editor area, Xcode 79
emulators 20
Enterprise edition, Xamarin Studio 9
Execute Disable (XD) 28

F

file inspector 77
File menu 46-48
files
  about 117
  Contents.json file 118
  Interface Builder (IB) file 118
  property list (PList) file 120
find navigator 76
FinishedLaunching() function 146

G

General tab, iOS Build pane
  options 62
GenyMotion
  about 30
  URL 30, 37
GNU Debugger (GDB) 162
Google Cloud Messaging service
  about 120
  reference link 121
Google Play Developer Program
  about 17-19
  subscribing 20
Google Play Store
  Additional Graphics 213
  Android application, publishing to 212-214
  App Description 212
  Application Type 212
  App Name 212
  App Screenshot 213
  Category 212
  Company Name 212
  Launcher Icons 212
  Support Information 212
  Video Link 213
Google Services Framework
  about 120
  reference link 121
Gorilla Testing 183

H

HAXM (Hardware Acceleration Execution Manager)
  about 28
  installing 28
Help menu
  about 56, 57
  API Documentation 57
  Open Log Directory 57
  Report a bug 57

I

IBOutlet 81
IDE 39
identity inspector 78

inactive state, iOS application lifecycle 144
INavigation interface 126
Indie edition, Xamarin Studio 8
Indie license 124
Information pads 44-46
Instruments 12, 161, 179
Integrated Development Environment. *See* IDE
Intel x86 Atom System Image
  about 26
  installing 27
Interface Builder 79
Interface Builder (IB) file 118
Interface Builder, Xcode 74
iOS 3.5-inch Retina display screenshots 218
iOS 4-inch Retina display screenshots 218
iOS 6.1 Simulator
  installing 21
iOS application
  creating 41
iOS application deployment
  build configuration 189
  build configuration, defining 189
  bundle signing 190
  distribution provisioning profile 185
  performing 184
iOS application icons 217
iOS application lifecycle
  about 144
  active state 145
  AppDelegate class 145
  background state 145
  examining 149
  inactive state 144
  not running state 144
  suspended state 145
  UIViewController lifecycle methods 147
iOS application, publishing
  about 190
  application page, creating 191-194
  binary, uploading 194, 195
  iTunes Connect account, setting up 191
iOS Apps Developer Program 184
iOS Binding Project 116
iOS Build pane
  Advanced tab 63, 64
  General tab 62

iOS control types
  URL 120
iOS Developer Program
  subscribing 18
iOS device
  testing 177
iOS devices, setting up
  about 31
  development certificate, obtaining 31, 32
  devices, provisioning 32
iOS interface, Xamarin Studio Designer
  about 87
  design surface 88
  Document Outline pad 88
  Properties box 88
  Toolbox pane 88
iOS iPad screenshots 219
iOS lifecycles
  examining 148, 149
iOS project templates
  about 110
  Empty Project 110
  iOS Binding Project 111
  iOS Library Project 112
  iOS Tabbed Application 110
  iOS Unit Tests Project 112
  iOS Utility Application 110
  Master-Detail Application 111
  OpenGL Application 112
  Page Based Application 111
  Single View Application 110
  Sprite-Kit Application 111
  Web View Application 111
iOS Provisioning Portal 185
iOS SDK
  about 11, 21
  installing 12
iOS simulator
  testing in 170-172
  tests, running 172
  working 173, 174
IParcelable interface 8
iPhone application
  creating, in Visual Studio 106-109
  working 109
issue navigator 76
iTunes 177

iTunes Connect
  about 190
  account, setting up 191
  reference link 191
  URL 191
iTunes University
  URL 37

J

Java Bindings Library 117
Java Native Interface (JNI) 117

L

Layout
  creating 96, 97
  working 97, 98
libraries
  about 115
  Binding Project 116
  Portable Class Library 115
Linker
  URL 62
Linker tab, Android Build pane
  options 65
log navigator 77
logs
  about 180
  crash logs 180
  debug logs 181

M

Mac App Development certificate
  creating 197, 198
Mac App ID
  registering 196, 197
Mac application deployment
  application configuration, setting 201
  build, for direct deployment 203
  build, for Mac App Store deployment 204
  developer certificates, installing 196
  Developer ID Certificate, creating 199
  development provisioning profiles,
    creating 200, 201
  direct deployment, signing for 202

Mac App Development certificate,
    creating 197, 198
Mac App ID, registering 196, 197
Mac App Store Certificates,
    creating 198, 199
Mac App Store deployment 205-207
Mac App Store deployment,
    signing for 203, 204
Mac OS X development machine,
    registering 199
performing 195
production provisioning profiles,
    creating 201
Mac Apps Developer Program 195
Mac App Store
    App Description 205
    App Name 205
    App Ratings 205
    App Screenshot 205
    Mac application, deploying to 205-208
Mac App Store Certificates
    creating 198
Mac App Store deployment
    build 204
    signing for 203, 204
Mac/Mac (open source) project templates
    about 114
    Empty Xamarin.Mac 115
    Xamarin.Mac 114
    Xamarin.Mac Document 115
    Xamarin.Mac Library 115
Mac OS X application screenshots 219
Mac OS X development machine
    registering 199
Make 60
makefile 60

N

NavigationPage class 126
navigation, Xamarin.Forms 126
navigator area, Xcode
    about 75, 76
    breakpoint navigator 77
    debug navigator 77
    find navigator 76
    issue navigator 76

log navigator 77
project navigator 76
symbol navigator 76
test navigator 77
Nexus 7 AVD
    creating, AVD Manager used 22, 23
NIB files 85
**not running state, iOS application
    lifecycle 144**

O

Objective Sharpie
    about 117
    reference link 117
OnActivated() function 145
OnCreate() method 153
OnDestroy() method 154
OnPause() method 154
OnResignActivation() function 146
OnRestart() method 153
OnRestoreInstance() 155
OnResume() method 153
OnSaveStateInstance() 155
OnStart() method 153
OnStop() method 154
Outlets
    about 80, 81
    adding 82

P

package manager,
        Android SDK Manager 93
Packaging tab, Android Build pane
    options 64
Portable Class Library (PCL)
    about 115
    using 115
Preferences
    Environment 69
    Other group 70
    Packages group 70
    Projects 69
    Source Code group 70
    Text Editor 69
    Version Control group 70

pricing plans
  URL 10
pricing structure
  about 9
  example company 10
private keystore, Android application
  creating 210
production provisioning profiles, Mac application
  creating 201
project editor 79
Project menu
  about 50
  Active Configuration 50
  Android Device Target 50
  Apply Policy… 50
  Create Package… 50
  Edit References… 50
  Export Policy… 50
  Generate Makefiles… 50
  Profile – Mono… 51
  Project Options 51
  Publish to TestFlight… 51
  Solution Options 51
  Zip App Bundle… 51
Project navigator 76
Project Options
  about 59
  Build group 60, 61
  General group 59, 60
  Run group 67
  Source Code group 68
  Version Control group 68
project templates
  about 110
  Android project templates 113
  iOS project templates 110
  Mac (open source) project templates 114
  Mac project templates 114
Properties pad. *See* Design pads
property list 79
property list (PList) file 120

Q

quick help inspector 78

R

Razor templating engine 117
ReleaseDesignerOutlets() method 86
resources, cross-platform developers
  third-party resources 37
  Xamarin resources 37
Run menu
  about 51-53
  Add Tracepoint 53
  Breakpoint 53
  Debug Application… 53
  Exceptions… 53
  Run Unit Tests 53
  Run With 53
  Start 52
  Step Into 53
  Step Out 53
  Step Over 53
  Stop 53
  Upload to Device 53

S

Samsung Galaxy S4 AVD
  creating, SDK and AVD Manager used 23-25
Search menu
  about 48, 49
  Go to File… 49
  Go to Type… 49
  Inspect 49
SGen garbage collection
  URL, for documentation 63
simulators 20, 169, 170
Size inspector 78
Solution Options
  about 57
  Build group 58
  General group 58
  Run group 58
  Source Code group 58
  Version Control group 58
Solution pad 42, 43
source control
  setting up 35, 36

source editor 79
Starter edition, Xamarin Studio 8
storyboard
  about 119
  creating 88-91
  working 91
STORYBOARD file 86
Subversion (SVN) 54
suspended state,
        iOS application lifecycle 145
symbol navigator 76
System.Data.SqlClient 8

T

table view cells 119
table view controllers 119
Team ID 185
test devices
  Android devices, setting up 33
  iOS devices, setting up 31
  setting up 30
TestFlight
  about 18, 178, 179
  account, setting up 178
  URL 178
testing
  considerations 181
  device testing 176
  performing, in Android emulator 174
  performing, in iOS simulator 170-172
test navigator 77
third-party AVD options 30
third-party resources, cross-platform
        developers 37
toolbar area, Xcode 75
Tools menu
  about 56, 57
  Insert Guid 56
  Launch Application Loader 56
  Launch Instruments 56
  Regex Toolkit... 56
  Sync with Xcode 56
  XML 56
Touch.Unit framework 164

U

UIViewController class
  ViewDidAppear() 148
  ViewDidDisappear() 148
  ViewDidLoad() 147
  ViewWillAppear() 148
  ViewWillDisappear() 148
UIViewController lifecycle methods
  about 147
  flowchart 147
Ultimate Widget Fu 183
unit test project
  creating 164, 165
unit tests
  about 163
  running 166-168
  URL 163
  working 168
utility area, Xcode
  about 77, 78
  attributes inspector 78
  connections inspector 78
  file inspector 77
  identity inspector 78
  quick help inspector 78
  size inspector 78

V

Version Control menu
  about 54, 55
  Checkout... 55
  Commit Solution 55
  Diff 55
  Log 55
  Merge Branch... 55
  Pop stash 55
  Push Changes... 55
  Rebase to Branch... 55
  Remove 55
  Stash... 55
  Switch to Branch 55
  Update Solution 55
view 119

view controller 119
ViewController
  adding, to project 83, 84
  working 84, 85
ViewDidAppear() event 148
ViewDidDisappear() method 148
ViewDidLoad() method 147
ViewGroup object 94
View menu
  about 48, 49
  Archives… 48
  Focus Document 48
  Show Disassembly 48
View object 94
ViewWillAppear() event 148
ViewWillDisappear() method 148
Virtual Machine (VM) 102
Visual Studio
  iPhone application, creating 106-108
Visual Studio 2012 Professional 103
Visual Studio plugin
  installation steps 105
  installing 102
  Mac, configuring 103
  requisites, for Mac 103
  requisites, for Windows 102
  Visual Studio toolbar, configuring 105, 106
  Windows machine, configuring 103
  Windows VM, configuring within Mac 104
Visual Studio toolbar
  configuring 105, 106

W

WillEnterForeground() function 146
WillFinishLaunching() function 146
WillTerminate() function 146
WindowManager 176
Window menu 56, 57
Windows 8 64-bit Pro 103

X

Xamarin.Android 11
Xamarin debugger 162
Xamarin Developer Center 37
Xamarin.Forms
  about 123

API design 126
  requisites 124
  URL 142
  XAML design 135
Xamarin.Forms application
  building, API design used 127-133
  building, XAML used 135-139
  working, with API 133, 134
  working, with XAML 141
Xamarin.Forms components
  about 125
  data binding 125
  navigation 126
  primary core components 125, 126
Xamarin.Forms project templates
  Blank App (Xamarin.Forms Portable) 124
  Blank App (Xamarin.Forms Shared) 124
  Class Library
    (Xamarin.Forms Portable) 124
Xamarin.Forms XAML
  about 135
  using 135-140
Xamarin Forums
  about 37
  URL 37
Xamarin Heapshot Memory Profiler
  URL 62
Xamarin.iOS 11
Xamarin.Mac 11, 114
Xamarin resources, cross-platform
    developers 37
Xamarin's Bugzilla
  about 37
  URL 37
Xamarin Studio
  Android application, creating 42
  development components, installing 11
  file 117
  installing 14-16
  iOS application, creating 41
  Layout, creating 96, 97
  libraries 115
  project templates 110
  source control, setting up 35
  storyboard, creating 88, 89
  URL 14
  Visual Studio plugin, installing 102

**Xamarin Studio Designer,
  for Android** 95, 96
Xamarin Studio Designer, for iOS 87, 88
Xamarin Studio IDE
  about 39-41
  Application menu 46-48
  Build menu 51-53
  Design pads 43, 44
  Edit menu 46-48
  File menu 46-48
  Help menu 56, 57
  Information pads 44-46
  Preferences 68
  Project menu 50
  Project Options 59
  Run menu 51-53
  Search menu 48, 49
  Solution Options 57
  Solution pad 42, 43
  Tools menu 56, 57
  Version Control menu 54, 55
  View menu 48, 49
  Window menu 56, 57
Xamarin Studio menu. *See* **Application
  menu**
Xamarin Studio platform options
  about 10
  Xamarin.Android 11
  Xamarin.iOS 11
  Xamarin.Mac 11
Xamarin Studio pricing plans
  about 8
  Business 9
  Enterprise 9
  Indie 8
  pricing structure 9
  Starter 8
Xamarin team
  URL 37
Xcode
  about 11, 12, 74
  debug area 79
  editor area 79
  installing 12
  installing, from App Store 12
  installing manually 13, 14
  Interface Builder 74
  navigator area 75, 76
  toolbar area 75
  utility area 77, 78
Xcode Installation
  finishing 14
Xcode installer
  URL 13
XIB files 85

About Packt Publishing

Packt, pronounced 'packed', published its first book "*Mastering phpMyAdmin for Effective MySQL Management*" in April 2004 and subsequently continued to specialize in publishing highly focused books on specific technologies and solutions.

Our books and publications share the experiences of your fellow IT professionals in adapting and customizing today's systems, applications, and frameworks. Our solution based books give you the knowledge and power to customize the software and technologies you're using to get the job done. Packt books are more specific and less general than the IT books you have seen in the past. Our unique business model allows us to bring you more focused information, giving you more of what you need to know, and less of what you don't.

Packt is a modern, yet unique publishing company, which focuses on producing quality, cutting-edge books for communities of developers, administrators, and newbies alike. For more information, please visit our website: www.packtpub.com.

Writing for Packt

We welcome all inquiries from people who are interested in authoring. Book proposals should be sent to author@packtpub.com. If your book idea is still at an early stage and you would like to discuss it first before writing a formal book proposal, contact us; one of our commissioning editors will get in touch with you.

We're not just looking for published authors; if you have strong technical skills but no writing experience, our experienced editors can help you develop a writing career, or simply get some additional reward for your expertise.

Xamarin Cross-platform Application Development

ISBN: 978-1-84969-846-7 Paperback: 262 pages

Develop production-ready applications for iOS and Android using Xamarin

1. Write native iOS and Android applications with Xamarin.
2. Add native functionality to your apps such as push notifications, camera, and GPS location.
3. Learn various strategies for cross-platform development.

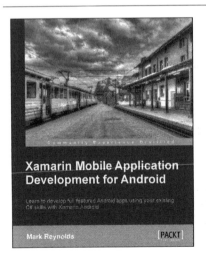

Xamarin Mobile Application Development for Android

ISBN: 978-1-78355-916-9 Paperback: 168 pages

Learn to develop full featured Android apps using your existing C# skills with Xamarin.Android

1. Gain an understanding of both the Android and Xamarin platforms.
2. Build a working multiview Android app incrementally throughout the book.
3. Work with device capabilities such as location sensors and the camera.

Please check **www.PacktPub.com** for information on our titles

Xamarin Mobile Application Development for iOS

ISBN: 978-1-78355-918-3 Paperback: 222 pages

If you know C# and have an iOS device, learn to use one language for multiple devices with Xamarin

1. A clear and concise look at how to create your own apps building on what you already know of C#.
2. Create advanced and elegant apps by yourself.
3. Ensure that the majority of your code can also be used with Android and Windows Mobile 8 devices.

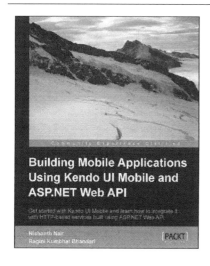

Building Mobile Applications Using Kendo UI Mobile and ASP.NET Web API

ISBN: 978-1-78216-092-2 Paperback: 256 pages

Get started with Kendo UI Mobile and learn how to integrate it with HTTP-based services built using ASP.NET Web API

1. Learn the basics of developing mobile applications using HTML5 and create an end-to-end mobile application from scratch.
2. Discover all about Kendo UI Mobile, ASP.NET Web API, and how to integrate them.
3. Understand how to organize your JavaScript code to achieve extensibility and maintainability.

Please check **www.PacktPub.com** for information on our titles

Made in the USA
Lexington, KY
07 March 2015